FlexOnomics + ThinkOnomics *with* *Dentonomics* 101

Thoughts
└ about;
Thinking
└ about;
└ Success!!
["by design"]

An opt-in on "**HOW TO PREVAIL . . . AND NOT JUST SURVIVE.**"

donald jay denton

ISBN: 146352112X
ISBN-13: 9781463521127

APPENDIX / CONTENT

Dedication **v**

Forward **vii**

Acknowledgement **ix**

Preface **xi**

Chapters as follows:

I. Concept wisdom for a foundation of success. **1**

II. Shrewd street sense ideas for marketing and business success, plus good fortune. **15**

III. Financial and Economic common sense ideas to create wealth, and preserve success. **35**

IV. Government, $'s, Politicians, YOUR money [The Observers, Regulators, Pipers.] **55**

V. Awareness of legalities and rules that one must learn to use and live with. **71**

VI. Tomorrow will soon be today, and it can be today's future. **99**

VII. Epilogue (Not to be overlooked.) **119**

*** Within the tomorrow text; note charts, graphs, and generic sample legal points and items of interest. ***

Dedication:

First, to individuals that gave this person the opportunities to have key turning points in life.

Adv. Dad Lewis – Temple Chapter DeMolay / Akron, OH.
Dr. George Knepper – History Prof. / Akron University
Clifford Thompson – Lutheran Brotherhood Life Ins.
George Knight – Pitney Bowes / Mansfield, Ohio
Col. Ken Cole – Executive / Boy Scouts of America
James Allen – United Negro College Fund
Mayor Sensenbrenner – Columbus, Ohio
Tom Byrnes – Executive / Connecticut General Life
Larry Wilson – Counselor Seller Training
Jerry Syi – Delta Life / Manhattan Funds
Howard Franz – President of Central Ohio Blue Cross
Dr. Robert Littler – Athens, Ohio
Harold Wiseman – Independent Ins. Agt., Gallipolis, Ohio
Rev. Banks – Clearfield, PA. Methodist Church
Russell Jay – Grandfather / Farmer / Eastern States Grain
Atty. Renee' Wormser / Atty. Michael Maher
Atty. Phillip Heckleling / Atty. Edward Schlessinger
Atty. David Cornfeld / Atty. James Hopple

T's a fact, there are many others, but the others remain undisclosed and nameless. The following phrase quoted here will make the point, and clearly explain why.

"No man is completely worthless, for he can always be used as a horrible example."

Most of these horrible examples were often quite brilliant and talented, but just never learned how to use their talent. The underlining fault was that they were in one way or another too greedy, "educated beyond their intelligence," suffered from "analysis paralysis," and worst yet "believed their own bull-shit."

This often meant that they had big mythical egos within their own mind of self-importance; - Too Bad!!

FORWARD:

Please take note: This is not a novel, and it is definitely not an academic thesis. The book is more of a categorized and sectionalized composite of down to earth short commentaries, and short illustrative stories to make key points. There will also be many bullet points of wisdom provided by a lot of brilliant people with great thoughts and ideas based upon their life experiences.

All the bullet points have legitimate psychological underpinnings, are quite self-explanatory, and are designed to assist reasonable maturing individuals who desire success in this life. This author only wants to provide you the 'Stepping Stones.'

"Isn't it strange that princes and kings
And clowns that caper in sawdust rings,
And common folks like you and me
Are makers of eternity?"

"To each of us is given a bag of tools,
A shapeless mass and a book of rules;
And each must make ere life has flown,
A stumbling block, or a stepping stone."

The knowledge that follows will be the ticket that allows one to play the game, and prevail. "For success comes in small cans; like a lot of I can do decisions."

Yet along the way, one may often stumble and make mistakes, but if that is not the case, then they are not trying their best at reaching out for success.

FORWARD

Acknowledgement:

TO

The leveler, balancer, cheerleader and
major backbone supporter of MOI !!

Magdalene C. Sarac
[Mrs. Magdalene C. Denton]

Thank You!!
donald j. denton

Additional Acknowledgement
to *the great*
writers, speakers, thinkers
* * * *A. Anonymous* * * *
[Even with all their appreciated mixed metaphors, colloquialisms, and their punctuation errors, they were always in the right place; - *for wiser persons to ignore.*]

This is an educational non-fiction work as related to practical street sense and class room knowledge and experiences around business, marketing, government, finance and law. Please seek the advice and legal counsel of a 'competent' attorney before considering application of any legal points shown within the book. Note that any resemblance to persons living or dead is purely coincidental.

Acknowledgments

PREFACE:

The purpose of this book is to give individuals **(you)** out there playing the game, the "Professional Edge." *Sadly,* we often do not know, what we do not know. Therefore, a person's judgments are no better than their known information. So to start with, do not dilute yourself with inhibition caused by other people's criticisms, sarcasms, aspersions and negativism. The anxiety these idiot people may create can paralyze one's perception of things around them.

Note that doubt is good. Doubt is often essential for progress, for it forces one to double check their confidence with past experiences. The fact is, doubt is often essential for progress, for one needs to move on from doubt to certainty by stepping forward with their confidence. Rather than stepping forward with insecurity, temptations, ignorance, and greed. It is therefore clear that success lies in muddling through uncertainty. ***Yet,*** the major stumbling blocks to success are the *fear of rejection*, and the *fear of failing.* So for *success,* one must have the capacity to fail, - without crumbling.

There is another key point to be made if one is to prevail and have a successful life. That becomes the issue of learning ***how to deal with unanticipated change***. This becomes easy once you realize that, "One can not direct the wind, but one can adjust the sails."

The fact is, "It is as you wish it!!" **Yet,** "Most people want to arrive; they just do not want to take the trip."

There is one pure fact, and that is, success has a price. The question becomes what price you are willing to pay to meet your goals, and achieve your wants, desires, needs and stated objectives. Please note that goals are a wonderful thing, but for heaven's sake, please do not put restrictive and stated time frames on your goals. Except one, you would like to "Achieve instant success in twenty-five years or less." Most of the time there are "no improper goals in life, only improper time frames." The best stated goal should be, "Do one's best every day, one day at a time;"- Period!

Within the following chapters, you will quickly learn how never to play in another man's ball game, or under their pre-claimed set of rules. A caution should be noted that you're always in danger when dealing with someone smarter than you. So when in a competitive or confrontational situation, you as a professional must lead others into playing the game within your arena. Remember this, that for you to succeed and be a winner, others will have to fail. Another harsh way of putting it might be, "To wound a king and not kill him, leaves one in big trouble."

This now brings to mind one good illustrative story:

* The Spider and the Fly (Excerpts) - By: Mary Howitt *

"Will you walk into my parlour?" Said the Spider to the Fly.

"The way into my parlour is up a winding stair. I've a many curious things to shew when you are there. > {*Oop's*!! – "Who goes up your winding stairs can ne'er come down again."}

"Will you rest upon my bed?" > {Oop's!! – "They never-never wake again who sleep upon your bed."}

Said the cunning Spider: "Dear friend what can I do, - to prove the warm affection I've always felt for you? I have within my pantry good store of all that's nice." > {Oop's!! -- "That cannot be, for that within your pantry, one had best not wish to see."}

"Sweet creature; - You're witty and you're wise, with handsome pearl and silver wings, and diamond brilliant eyes!" {Oop's!! – "Soon the Fly; hearing these wily, flattering words, came slowly flitting by; -- poor foolish thing."}

"And now to those who may this story read: I pray you heed the lesson learned; -> Unto some wise and thoughtful counsel heard. Close not the heart and ear and eye; -> And take a lesson from the tale, of the Spider and the Fly."

My grandmother Jay may have said it all in a shorter better way with; - - *"Love many, trust few, and learn to paddle your own canoe."*

But the bottom line remains the same, and always will be: It will be your "attitude, not your aptitude" that will make you successful once you have gained sufficient knowledge and experience. So remember that, - - - - ***"Enthusiasm without knowledge, - is like running in the dark."***

Otherwise, one's potential success might well get caught up in a real trapping web for the benefit of other's consumption.

CHAPTER I

Concept wisdom for a foundation of success.

One of the best quotes to get the ball rolling comes from the "Man from LaMancha" as written by Cervantes:

"With imagination men fulfill their dreams. You must follow your quest, - love not what you are, - but what you will become. So!! See life as it should be, - not as it is"

Fact is that success only arrives by being confident in one's self. That confidence will only come first with basic knowledge, and the application of doing with trial and error experiences. Since motivation without substance will only lasts a limited amount of time. One must then have a magnetic compelling purpose to pay their dues for obtaining success. Yes, one's "enthusiasm is contagious, but whatever it is that one has is also contagious."

The effort at learning is to interrogate the past words of wisdom from the prologue past which may well be useable today. A good future comes from capitalizing upon other people's creative and inspiring thoughts and ideas; - then by cultivating upon other people's seeds of wisdom. But as Emerson stated, "Do not follow the past." Therefore, one will then hopefully benefit by producing a better and more efficient game plan in the tomorrows for achieving personal success.

But in doing so, learn not to mistake bull-crap for fertilizer, and how to separate the Silver Chalice from the Wooden Priest. So be forewarned that there will be many who will try to lead you down the "Prim Rose Path" or the fantasy "Yellow Brick Road," but too often it turns out to be that *the* "Road to hell is paved with good intentions." That is why success quite often means being a contrarian. So one will soon learn in this life that talk is cheap, and small change takes the bus. Therefore, start judging people by the way they walk, and not by the way they talk. A pastor once said: "A man of words and not of deeds is like a garden full of weeds." That is why a person's fame standing alone cannot be equated to mean that the person is a success in this life.

Note that being truthful and factual is not always politically correct, but under all circumstances one must remain honest, truthful, and keep their word even if it hurts. Pascal may have stated it best:

"Truth is never a lost cause, even though it may hurt, and few things hurt more than the truth."

But the fair warning is that one should first put their brain and mouth in gear, and then count to ten; before stating facts and/or opinions.

Maybe a definition of success issued by Albert Einstein may help:

> "If **A** equal success, then the formula
> is **A** equals **X** *plus* **Y** *plus* **Z**.
> **X** is work. **Y** is play. Z is ...
> ... keep your mouth shut."

Now we add in a quote to the recipe by Maya Angelou:

> "People will forget what you said,
> people will forget what you did,
> but people will never forget ...
> ... how you made them feel."

Therefore, the object is to do your best, by not getting caught up in minor and immaterial things. To do so proves that one of the great enemies in the world of both man and nature is stagnation. Haven't you ever noticed water in a still pool that smells and is loaded with pestilence? Therefore the question becomes: "Wouldn't you rather be frustrated than bored?"

The basic fact will be, once you're prepared, is to realize that there are only two basic key assets for success.

One: *People*; - here one must learn how to evaluate and deal with all types of individuals with varying personality types. And note that *people do not care how much you know, until they know how much you care.* That is why it is often stated that the two most important words in marketing are to

"Service First." So be receptive, listen, and then you will know everything you know; plus everything they know. Yet sadly, as you will quickly learn, most people do not really know what they want out of life; - but they do know that they have not gotten it yet.

Two*: Time;* - This means making the best use of your time. You must learn to weed out window shoppers, freeloaders, sponge people and temperamental idiots. One should learn that you can always tell the size of a person, by the size of the things that make them mad. Then use time to study and learn from others; all while staying current and up-to-date. Next, follow the Boy Scout motto of -"Be Prepared!" Since one can not accomplish and procrastinate at the same time (or put another way, one can not huff and puff, blow out and suck in at the same time), never forget that change is constant, and the secret is to adapt, not adopt. That is why one must always be prepared, and learn when to go stage left or stage right on very short notice. These dance moves are often a necessity in one's life to remain successful.

Just remember; that in life, the little mistakes you can absorb, but the big mistakes will absorb you. Yet do not let apprehension and fear absorb you; for you must learn to do what you fear, or fear is in control. At this point Ralph Waldo Emerson may have said it best: "Fear not evil, that has not yet arrived."

Now at this point, one has to receive a reminder from Macbeth:

> "Out, out, brief candle! Life's but a walking shadow,
> a poor player, that struts and frets his hour upon the
> stage, and then is heard not more."

Fact is: A decision not to make a decision, is a decision by default, and that makes one a "Mug Wamp." The "Mug Wamp" is a fence sitter in life who always has his "Mug" on one side of the fence, and his "Wamp" on the other side of the fence. The basic reason for why, is the Wamp's fear of failure. Sad, for success is what happens when you flunk failure, and it is referred to as failing forward. That is why one must realize early on that they do not explode into success, but grow into success. Gustave Flauber may have said it best: *"Talent is a long patience."*

But this romantic realist also said something else of great importance: *"Even the slightest thing contains a little something that is unknown."* And for success, one's job is to find out what that little something is. This usually involves a lot of creative thinking, and continually thinking outside of the box.

There was this outstanding motivation speaker, Herb Somebody, who spoke at a major marketing conference. His introductory overhead was short sweet and blunt. It read, "How to become dumb ass successful with;

- A few good common sense rules.
- A little selective knowledge.
- Ignorant avoidance by knowing the questions to ask.
- And knowing who not to trust.

Then he went on for two hours to make all his points, and to clearly prove all his points. This all based upon his wisdom that he gleaned from others in past times smarter than himself. His points will be clearly dispersed throughout this book on how to prevail and not just survive within your chosen endeavors of life.

Lewis Carroll stated it best in "Through the Looking Glass:"

"It takes all the running you can do, to say in the same place." This is definitely true when you consider all the responsibilities in life one has to deal with on a daily basis. So try to relax and accept the fact that *life is often routine panic*. That is why when struggling for success; one must always be extending themselves, and at times needing to push the envelope.

But fair warning; - never go to the razor's edge. For life is too short, and one often needs time to take a moment too smell the flowers along the way. A wise man once said: "It is not important that you came to work early, or that you left work late, - but why?" Everyone should put a lot of thought into that comment. So maybe it is time for my daily prayer that one may feel free to use in moments of stress and bewilderment.

> "So far today, Lord, I've done all right. I haven't
> gossiped, haven't lost my temper, haven't been greedy,
> or grumpy, nasty, or self-centered."
> "I'm really glad about that. But in a few minutes, Lord,
> I'm going to get out of bed, and then I'm going too need
> a lot of help.
>
> Thank You!"

Now that the necessary psychological underpinnings are in place, it is time to present the following before covering some "Basic Rules of the Road." **First** this obvious *tongue in check* sense of gratitude, with an...

> ... "Ode to Incompetency & Ignorance."
> [This Ode is about people you should not, - love to hate.]

The people you just have to love if you're in the marketing game for profit. Be it finance, insurance, law, aluminum siding, or used cars and Amway. For in this game the object is; "To make the fish chase the boat." Here is where most "people fish" always end up baiting their own hook to get reeled into the Charlie Tuna can.

Yet, how can they be identified?!?! Here is where Pearl Bailey gave us one of the clues: "When people have to wear a sign around their neck to say who they are, - they ain't."

Easy!- you just have to love those people who were born on third base, then thought and believed that they hit a triple. Small package people.

Also one has to love people that are inflicted with Ph.d-idus, and have never realized that they were "educated beyond their intelligence. Then they go out to prove to others that they have the "I.Q. of a Tulip."

Yet, one just has to love those people who come into your office with fear and panic written all over their face, and heard in their voice; - So that one can now triple their fee on the promise to try and relieve their desperation, fear and insecurity.

But one really has to love people motivated by greed, and the quick buck. So now one really gets the sucker fish on the bait line; plus loving to devour them dearly, when they claim to fear and hate the Internal Revenue Service. You know; those identifiable greedy people who prefer tax evasion, rather than legal tax avoidance. Yes, the idiot individuals that have just never realized that people, who will lie for you, will also lie to you. DU!!

Therefore one needs to appreciate all those "Self-Made Men" who believe and worship their Creator. Sad, for they always end up believing their own bull feather press clippings. Yet anyone can easily manipulate them by blowing smoke in their face, and up their backside. The sad part is that most of these types of individuals' think they have value, and are irreplaceable; I do not think so. Fact is, everyone is expendable and replaceable. The proof is in the water. Go fill up a cup full of water, then put your finger down in the water, and leave it in there for a few seconds. Okay! - Now slowly remove the finger out of the cup of water, and look at the hole it leaves. DU!!

It is practically a necessity that one appreciates horny people who are stupid, and don't know it. They will make you a fortune if you never trust them. You know them well; they think with their zipper, and drink too much Scotch, beer and Martinis. All this while going through male metaphase starting at about age fifty as annoying loud mouths at the Country Club. Or whatever, with the new sports car, and the new chick-a-dee who is an actuary in love with their handsome leather wallet with a higher mortality factor.

Everyone just loves people who never, never learned, to never play in another man's ball game, and then they stupidly continue to underestimate their opponent/competition. But many of these people are ignorant, and certainly often blissful. They generally will never prevail even with common sense, or valid horse sense; even if it comes with three quarters of "Stable Thinking." Just look at Las Vegas and Atlantic City; they call them gamblers, and the real loser they call whales. You know the one's with a lot of blubber that get harpooned, and often beach themselves.

Yet one really has to dislike window shoppers and procrastinators. These are usually people who do not control 51% of their social, economic, and business lives; - but act as if they do. The worst in this category are usually older middle management wan-a-be's. They can make everyone's lives interesting and miserable, and love that phony word of power; - "*Seniority.*"

Now should one really think about it; would they really want everyone else to be very competent? The whole profit concept is like planned obsolescence, for incompetency makes us all money. It makes our services necessary, and makes the economic world go around. But if everyone was competent, everyone might well be financially harmed. Which means you and most everyone else might be poorer?!?!

Facetious conclusion: There needs to be a poorer system for education, more in-breeding, more people with the "Little Jack Horner" syndrome, and more politicians to keep the system screwed up. Reminds one of a simple opportunity verse; "In my own little corner, in my own little chair; I can be whatever I want to be now." *** B11030 ***

King Lear asked an interesting question: "Is man no more than this?" This now reminds one of an old German saying: "Too soon old, too late smart." So it is my hope that anyone reading this work does not wish to have Saint Jude as their patron saint, for he is the Saint of Lost Causes.

But sadly, and not to anyone's sudden surprise; there exist within our environment numerous ignorant self-centered and self-absorbed egoistic homo-sapien fruitcakes. Those people who will resent your success, and wish you failure. So one must learn to avoid, ignore, and quickly set these misfits aside. Then fire them out of your life; for one can not get hung up with loser friendships that do not contribute, but will only drain energy from you. No matter how nice these people are, you cannot allow them to hold you back or bring you down; regardless of the guilty feelings you may incur because of your relationships and friendships.

The basic kindergarten rules of the road are simple and clear. So you must first recognize what stage of growth development you're lingering within.

Will that be as the, - -

- Unconscious / Incompetent
  or the ╬ * Area of ...
- Conscious / Incompetent ╬... avoidance behavior.
  or the
- Unconscious / Competent
  or the
- Conscious / Competent?

The trailer follow-up to these previous points, for giving one valid self-status evaluation, will be further clarified within the marketing section. That diagramed illustration will groom one to achieve the professional edge at listening and empathizing, by indentifying and knowing the human personality nature of the potential client, or that date sitting in front of you. This is often referred to as "Controlled Power Selling."

The insight there provided can certainly be applicable to a pastor or rabbi trying to convince members of a congregation to take certain action, like run a building development fund. The system definitely applies to charities with professional personnel trying to recruit volunteers who will donate valuable time, and even money. Plus, there is no question it applies totally within the business world arena of marketing, advertizing, and finance. Specifically when one must know how to control their environment, know their priorities, and how to direct other people's percentage of affect upon profits.

Then you will clearly understand this formula:

L.B. + A.I. + T.J. = SUCCESS! { Answer will be deferred }:

There are a few additional rules of the road for success, and some were lessons most likely learned from experiences in one's youth. These learned lessons have value, for they show one how to deal with humanity's hemorrhoids.

1. The height of irresponsibility, - is when one accepts the responsibility for other people's irresponsibility.
2. Never hit a man in the jaw who chews tobacco.
3. Do not be too quick to forgive or forget. Be time wise patient, and never get mad and lose your center. Never attack, just snare the offender as with the "Spider and the Fly."
4. It is often much easier to ask forgiveness, than get permission.
5. Only help those who are willing to help themselves, for you are not your brother's keeper. Yet, it is best to let someone else provide the second chance, just in case the leopard does not change its spots.
6. You must decide in life whether you're going to be a Profit Center or have a Non-profit life style. Don't let Goodie-to-Shoe people blind side you with guilt, for many people are not worth saving. So as the Bible wisdom so clearly states; "Prune the Vine."
7. Remember that a bee with honey in its mouth has a stinger in his tail. Also take note, that compromise is like asking the cannibals to eat you last.
8. Please note that the body is 90% water, and only 10% matter. Therefore, you must decide whether you want to be a person or a puddle.

9. Never apply your moral judgments' and ethical standards to clients or competition. Do not judge, even if you have been there. But biblically you have the right to be a fruit inspector; "You shall know them by their fruits." *So the key is to* "Separate the wheat from the chaff."
10. Always make the bully or over-confident jerk pay a price after crossing over into your space to offend or cause harm. They may be the winner, but leave them damaged with second thoughts.
11. Take note: That they who panic first, panic best. > Opportunity!!
12. There is nothing wrong with losing, for it is a learning experience that you had better capitalize upon. The object at worst should be to create a stalemate.

Now for that # that nobody likes, and would first prefer black cats while walking under ladders, but this # has a great point to be made.

13. "Today is the only cash you have, so spend it well. For yesterday is a cancelled check, and tomorrow is only a promissory note."

This point may well have been expressed in a better way 300 years ago by a Japanese samurai as written within the book of "Hagakure:"

"Understand that life consists only of the present moment. The past exists only as memory, and the future only as imagination. There is surely nothing other than the single purpose of the present moment. A man's whole life is a succession of moments after moments. If one fully understands the present moment there will be nothing else to do, and nothing else to pursue. So live being true to the single purpose of the moment."

That is why the Roman Emperor Marcus Auerelius stated: "That whether one dies young or old, it is the same; for one loses the only thing one has or ever will have, - the present moment."

Now let's move up to our modern age where Louis Seltzer says: "I live for tomorrow. I can scarcely wait until it comes. To be sure, yesterday was interesting. Of course, today is the immediate challenge. But tomorrow is for the plans, for the dreams, and for the reaching up."

So with that we must move on, and in doing so remember that "Fame is fleeting." Yes, some get their fifteen minutes of fame, but very, very few get 15, 20 or 25 years of fame. These few lucky ones remembered that change is constant, learning is forever, and you must strive to become what you commit yourselves to. If not, the weakness shown today enslaves us tomorrow.

Therefore we are required to be different, be uncommon, and reach a little farther beyond what is possible; to be an uncommon person, for common people go nowhere. No apologies for this fact of life, for worker bees and soldier ants are a predominate necessity. They are the needed labor force, since few followers are ambitious enough to be the chief, or the leader of the pack. Most people prefer complacency and contentment rather then paying the struggling and hardworking price for success.

So as the uncommon individual, you must go beyond that which is expected, and have vision. Sure, there is always that sense of fear and insecurity when one sticks their neck out, but "Behold the Turtle; - It can only make progress when it sticks its neck out." And yes, some people always seem to appear strong and confident, but secretly over and above their outward confidence they often have an insecure fear of failing. Yet, all fairy tales do have an ending; so if one starts losing their confidence, they will start losing interest, and the fairy tale ending may not be so nice.

One must always appreciate the words of Dr. Haggii when he stated; "Oh Lord, - do not let me die, until I am dead." So a good follow up question for one to think deeply about is; "What if I make a mistake by living?"

Therefore it may be wise for one to remember these words of wisdom before moving on to the Business, Marketing, Finance, Government, Law and your life's tomorrow section; - "The winner will be the one who comes out of the Bear Cave alive."

The bear cave is the learning experience, but many a soul never exits the bear cave to beneficially learn from the experience. Therefore, while presenting how to exist the bear cave alive, some points in the following material may seem to have a bit of negative overtones. Nothing could be farther from the truth, for the points are presented simply to show the many claws on the bear that could rip one apart while playing in this game of life. The desired object should be for one to successfully exit the bear cave alive, while remaining in one prevailing piece.

Of course, it does not help much if one exits the bear cave, and then gets sucked into a Black Hole of negativism and defeatism about failing forward to achieve success. So maybe the lyrics of an old song, along with proven related science of quantum mechanics, may help prove the necessary point. The verse of the song is as follows;

> "Accentuate the positive.
> Eliminate the negative.
> Latch onto the affirmative.
> Don't mess with Mister In-between"

Now even science supports this concept to help one stand out and separate themselves from the crowd. It often requires taking the bull by the horns, and then to gore the bear into submission or die. So as with atoms, electrons and neutrons, with their positives and negatives; it is now known that Black Holes only suck in the negatives. So then the positives separate and scatter away from the Black Hole's negativism to enjoy relative space again. So the obvious point is to accentuate the positive, then eliminate the negative, and latch onto the affirmative, in order to stay healthy, wealthy, and wise.

Oh but first, before we move on; - it is requested that one partakes in a five question comprehensive exam. The test is to prepare one for understanding the following chapters on business, finance, government and law issues that may cover and save one's rear-end. Knowledge with preventive medicine awareness will help one prevail, preserve, and maintain earned success.

Please try honestly to analyze the questions before looking ahead at what the answer or solution may be. - Thank you!

Question #1 > What is wrong with the following sentence?
. . . "San Pablo rode his burrow into town."

Question #2 > Please read the following sentence with comprehension, slowly and twice. Then look away, and answer the desired question.

"Traffic Safety is the result of many years of scientific study combined with the experience of many years."

* * * Now look away, - and tell us all how many letter f's are within the sentence?

Question #3 > What is wrong with this sentence? . . .

. . . "A possum has more teeth than any other North American Mammals."

Question #4 > Now this is a brain twister. How many words, without looking things up (In one minute; okay we'll give you three minutes.), can you write down as single words starting with the letter "Y." > ***Go!!***

Question #5 > What are the only two known mammals that do not get crippling arthritis in their joints, and why?

Now we will find out how well you did. So it must be comforting to know that you are the only one who will know the results. This quiz is like, for me to know, and you to find out.

The answer to question one was shown and based upon an Internal Revenue slide shown at a small business conference. The agent asked how many found the mistake, and then stated; "Those that did not find the mistake do not know their ass from a hole in the ground."

Most everyone misses the answer on question two with five, but you now know with your powers of observation, there are seven.

Now for question three, as to the proper spelling, how does one spell . . . opossum?

The best known record on and about the letter "Y" is seventeen.

The answer to question five is BATS and OPOSSUMS. The why is that they hang upside down.

So in closing this chapter, please be encouraged and believe in thyself. Do not ever, ever be inhibited by persons with fancy degrees, or where the degree was achieved. Since the most successful and smartest lawyers, accountants, business and finance majors graduated from no named or little named colleges and universities. Also it should be noted that the majority of the richest, wealthiest, successful people this author has known (not including individuals within the medical and dental profession, plus three large animal veterinarians'), did not have college or university degrees. They were self taught, ambitious, and quite aggressive. They had good street sense, and in addition that strange sixth sense wisdom.

One nice person who was personally known to me, barely finished high school with a C minus, for he had to work nearly full time to help support his widowed mother and three younger siblings. This guy had such a desire to learn, he purchased a complete Funk and Wagnall encyclopedia set from the local grocery store. He studied them day and night, and most people actually thought he had memorized them. Even with his mild speech impediment and his hidden unrecognized genius, he had the advantage over everyone by the time he was twenty-nine. The big why, was because he had great people skills, and really understood human nature.

This man started with little or nothing, and was ambitiously self educated. His high school counselor told him that he was not college material, and should become a factory squad worker at a local manufacturing plant. Yet the last time I saw him, his business success was worth about $28,000,000.00.

Therefore it is fitting to quote a few paraphrased excerpt lines from "The man in the Glass," or as often referred to as the "Man in the Mirror."

> "When you get what you want, and you're a king for the day;
>
> Go to the mirror and look at yourself, and see what that man has to say."
>
> "For the person whose judgment and verdict will count most in your life, will be the one staring back at you from the glass. The one whose judgment on you must pass."
>
> "Many a soul might say you're wonderful and great, but you hope the man in the glass will not say you're a bum. For he is the only one you need to please, never mind the rest."
>
> "Yeah! You may fool the whole world and get pats on your back, but your final reward will be heartache and tears; - If you've cheated the man in the glass. But you passed the most dangerous test if the person in the glass still remains your friend."

So as you the reader move forward, let's not forget the words of Macbeth, and replay them for you once more:

> "Out, out, brief candle! - Life is but a walking shadow,
> a poor player, that struts and frets his hour upon the
> stage, and then is heard no more."

Otherwise, one might be hearing the unwanted words of Gloucester:

> "As flies to wanton boys, are we to the Gods; -
> They kill us for their sport."

P.S. - As you progress through the following chapters, sections may seem occasionally deep, and slightly analytical. No apologies, for if you absorb the following knowledge, you will become the controller of the environments to which you intend to succeed. For all the following information has relative meaning and purposeful intent at assisting one **(you)** to become a leader of the pack, and not just as a devoted follower.

#

CHAPTER II

Street sense factors for marketing and business success.

Now that we'll be narrowing down the areas of economics and finance to the specifics relating to marketing and business, one needs to think about that time aged question of: "What came first, the chicken or the egg?" Now do not laugh, for all will become quite relevant when we start simplifying down with common sense and street sense those renowned macro economic theories. You know! Those in-house, academic, published, intellectual observer papers that add complicated sophistication to ordinary reason and common sense. But the fact is; it was good for all of us that we had these teachers. The ones some students often referred to as a bit weird or strange, but otherwise brilliant in the big picture scheme of explaining the macro world of economics.

Yet this now leads to another very important historical question of interest. That question is; "What is the oldest profession in the world?" Okay, you obviously guessed the right inappropriate answer, for that is what everyone tends to say; - prostitution! Not so, but it really is in the ball park. The oldest profession is financial planning based upon successful marketing and salesmanship. Yet some will still argue that it was fee for services. Then later entered the government interlopers to stop abuse, and limit somewhat the need for the 'caveat emptor' rule of "let the buyer beware."

Fact is, without marketing and salesmanship there are no successful businesses, for great production and development standing alone is just an empty suit. So take note: That if you have no buyers, you have no sales; if you have no sales, you have no income; and if you have no income, then there are no buyers. Wow!! It's John Hobson's 'Ripple Effect' economics, and this makes the trickle down Supply Side theory a little questionable as to its integrity. Yet, along with this, it is still enjoyable reading to explore figuratively fictitious Libertarianism, Lassie Faire with Adam Smith, and Princeton's theoretical Game Theory.

This is a new stringy and spacey game theory principle where some academic fantasy nerds are trying to connect 'Game Theory' with finance and economics. This Game Theory concept is way out in left field. For this idea to work, it requires that each party or all parties negotiating are reasonable and knowledgeable people. With the uncertainty issue not being a factor. But theory applications tend to bomb out in the future when written by historians of record, where acting only as observers, and not as participants in the world at play. Sadly, most of the published economic theorists tend to be analytical fundamentalists, not creative out of the box thinkers, and too-too often purveyors of doom.

Fact is, the world is controlled by goods and money, and there is only one God of success in business. That God is net cash flow profits. Therefore the most important words in business are Cash Flow, Cash Flow, and Cash Flow. You either have it, or you don't. Then one often hears economists claiming that the new normal with economics and finance is uncertainty. So what planet are these experts living on? Fact is, uncertainty has been and always will be, not surprisingly, around business situations with unexpected and annoying circumstances. These coming out of left field events may often seem overwhelming and unnecessarily time consuming; but all this in the end, is what makes business a challenge and enjoyable.

That is why one must learn from their mistakes, face up to failures, and analyze the failures. Then reach out, have faith, and try again; no longer being afraid of the failing risk factor. This track for success is referred to as failing forward, and while along the way learning how to overcome and accept rejection. Then the final winner will be those knowledge people with good people skills. The skills that tend to make one successfully rich and wealthy. It is the stabilizing beneficial reward as the price paid for having one's patience's and emotional stability occasionally tested and pushed to the limits.

As often stated: "Your life becomes effective, when you become effective." This very often deals with self-control. So as they also say; "You can always tell the size of a person, by the size of the things that make them mad." Now all this brings us to one very key issue in order to be successful in the business world, and that question at issue is; "How does one, being you, deal with unanticipated change?" A good example of this in today's Macro economic world is the shift away from labor cost. This labor cost containment shift has made the issue of labor a commodity. Now in conjunction with this, there has been a major economic shift toward the development of third world markets. So is it not strange, that some people ignorantly assumed the third world would stay a third world, and that they would not become major consumers with the added benefits of cheap labor?

These labor and third world issues are prime examples of narrow mindedness in thought along with poor future foresight; by spending too much time analyzing the past. They clearly read the tea leaves wrong. So for obtaining future success, think like Hamlet with his quote in Shakespeare; "All time is out of joint, and I was born to help set it right."

Let's take a moment to prove a point about being careful as to what you wish for. Today's circumstances were not a result of the big picture items as W.W.I, W.W.II, Korea or Vietnam. They were only indirect cause and effect events. First was a big blunder: The break up of the Ottoman Empire that still haunts our economics today, followed by the Balfour Treaty, and then the blunderbuss 1922 New World Mandate. The next bright lights were the innovation of technology, the G.I. Bill that made us smarter, and then our forgiving generosity with the MacArthur Plan and the Marshall Plan to rebuild Japan and Europe. This was all very nice since former enemies ended up having better and newer equipment and factories than we in the U.S. Then over time the men of the G.I. Bill participation became shrewd and wise business owners and corporate executives. They quickly learned about corporate profits, cash flow benefits, and the necessity for cost containment.

The developing end result was that technology started replacing mental labor. Next, automation started replacing physical labor. Then along came third world globalization that located cheaper labor and manufacturing cost. Now U.S. labor cost became a material issue of consequence. So what benefits are derived for a U.S. business man by maximizing technology and automation?

> No overtime pay. > No vacation pay. > No sick leave pay.
> No fringe benefit cost (health, medical, retirement, disability).
> No union. > No Americans with Disability Rights Act.
> No family leave issues. > No EEOC (equal employment issues).
> No Sexual Harassment issues > No Cobra Issues.

> No Social Security or Unemployment cost.
> No Workman's Compensation issues. > Fewer management and labor issues; while definitely having no Anti-discrimination issues. > Plus no costly issues pertaining to a National Health Care program.

All else left or remaining is now producing better thermo-dynamics as to production, performance, and accountability. Then WOW! One now gets the additional benefits of added value to cash flow with depreciation and amortization, government credits and incentives; plus far lower maintenance costs. Therefore, profit modernization requires that a business owner must always remember that ***"Employment is not adoption."*** Then always continue to evaluate the remaining employees' "percentage of affect upon profits." So the concept here should be quite obvious; it is referred to as the "key person replacement time factor." Replacement with what, by what, and by when?

Therefore, there has been no better time and opportunity than this current time, for people who have groomed their people skills. Skills developed by observing and absorbing everyone else's beneficial knowledge and experience. This means everyone. As stated previously; "No man is completely worthless, for he can always be used as a horrible example."

Therefore a key way to succeed in marketing and business is too make one's self near, or somewhat indispensable. Why? Because we as a society got what we wished for, and then too late realized that general labor has become dispensable and replaceable. Therefore, appreciate the fact that there is nothing replaceable about a top salesman or marketing executive that produces sales and creates revenue cash flow. These profit makers must be a Jack-of-all- trades, and specialize with one in particular, - People! This is why a top sales person is referred to as the "Man in the Arena," who knows their "unique factor" while being themselves. That factor in dealing with potential clients is knowing how to maximize the benefits, and minimize the cost; like taking the word 'ice' out of the word price. As so often stated; "A professional salesman is heard, but not seen." For it is not who you are, but who you make people think you are. This talent is a trial and error product, learned too often early on from heart rendering experiences. Yet that is the price one pays to become successful.

Now as for the wanting to be a successful business owner who provides products and/or services, the key objective at marketing "is to get the fish to chase the boat." All this while controlling internal cost and expenses. So now may be the appropriate time to remember good sound, solid, down to earth common sense farmer strategies learned down on the farm. As follows; - -

1. **You reap what you sow; or, ->** "What you sow, ye shall also reap."

   This deals with producing tomorrows result today. It also makes reference to future generations, for they will most certainly reap what we sow today. Therefore, the future may be limited by what we sow today. So it is important that one gets off their dead apathy, and then works to get their potential clients off their dead apathy. Yet the farmer knows that when one sows crops, that the crops need watering, hoeing, and fertilizing for successful results.

2. **The early bird gets the worm.**

   This means you do not punch the clock, and you're Johnny on the spot with more knowledge at work, than body at work. The point being that the early bird will succeed, while the late bird fails. It's so refreshing to know that many people mistake body odor for activity, and so too often violate others' rights by speaking more clearly than they think. We should pay these fool's a bonus for their ignorant help.

   Success here means to be visible where the action is, to stretch one's self, and pour one's self into the main stream. After that, do the very best you can, and then piss on it.

3. **A bird in the hand is worth two in the bush.**

   Here is where one should take note that a good referral is better than a cold calling prospecting list. So learn quickly that referrals are the inventory of one's successful business, not products.

4. **Don't count your chickens before they hatch.**

   This statement is quite obvious, but it brings back Elwood P. Dowl's saying in the play Harvey; "You can be oh so cleaver, or oh so smart; I recommend pleasant." Then this also suggests to one that spending requires revenue, cash, and an obligation to pay.

Something that seems to be missing from our society's economic ethics today.

This also points out there is always the exception, so always be prepare for the unexpected. The operative word is 'HOWEVER', for sometimes things just go wrong as with the "best laid plans of mice and men often go astray." It usually happens when we don't know what we don't know. Murphy's Law!!

5. **Save for a rainy day.**

That's right! "Be not a borrower or lender be." Particularly note the borrowing part in order to avoid compounding interest on the debt. Also in business one must learn to save by controlling cost and expenses. The following may be a good example?

I got this great idea early on; every Friday afternoon I took all my dirty dress shirt down to the Salvation Army. I donated the shirts to them, and then got my receipt for a nice big tax deduction. Note that it was just too costly to pay $2.50 to get each one cleaned, pressed, and starched at the neighbor laundry mat. Now, the first thing on the following Monday morning, I went back to the Salvation Army and purchased back my nice clean, pressed and starched dress shirts for fifty-cents each. Okay, it's meant to make a humorous point.

6. **Get your ducks in a row.**

Two technical terms for successfully marketing one's business are; ***Retention;*** - Keep what we got. ***Acquisition,*** - Get the rest. As the farmer also said; "Cows do not give milk, you must take it from them twice a day." The stumbling block here is that business owner's tend to work in their business, but not on their business.

They also planned well for going into business, but forgot to plan at all for going out of business. A major problem! Again, the business owner must focus on his markets like a laser, and not on products.

Yet, I've often wanted to say to a client; "Sir, have you ever considered having a wisdom tooth put in?" But I restrained myself, realizing this thought; "Why pay more, for most people's thoughts aren't worth a penny." Proving that one can not be all things to all people, and one definitely does not want to work for everyone.

7. **Don't put all your eggs in one basket.**

The why is that life is often routine panic. So the only safety net is diversification, and then quickly learning when to go stage left or stage right on very short notice. So the key is to adapt, but not to adopt.

8. **You can't make a silk purse out of a sow's ear.**

Like the dog in the manger; it won't eat the hay, but it will not let the cows eat it either. This also points out the fact that one can not win them all, but on the other hand, you don't want to win them all. For when a client's problems become more important to you, than to them; you no longer have a client. Walk away!

That is why Colonel Sanders and KFC did not start off selling dead chickens to the public. They only sold "finger lick'en good.

9. **Don't let the foxes guard the henhouse.**

I do not think this needs much of an explanation. As long as one makes a note to themselves that evil, sin, greed and power grabbing operates twenty-four seven throughout the year, and every year. So now we all must remember that nice Russian potato farmer carrying home in the bitter cold winter a heavy bag of potatoes for his family to live and survive. He then heard this little bird chirping loudly, and near death in the freezing snow.

Farmer picked up the bird, took off his gloves, and tried to warm up the bird in his warm hands. But he could not carry the bird and the bag of potatoes at the same time. He then saw a big pile of warm moose dropping, created a little hole, and put the bird down into the warm dropping to stay warm and survive. Wow! The bird revived itself in the warm moose dropping, and started chirping loudly with joy. Oop's! A nearby wolf heard the chirping, came over to the bird in the moose dropping, and being hungry chomped down and ate the nice little bird.

The moral of this story is; that the one who puts you in it may not necessarily be your enemy, and the one who takes you out of it may not necessarily be your friend.

10. **Separate the wheat from the chaff.**

    A must that is necessary both inside and outside of one's business is in knowing who to separate from. Therefore know that in every situation there is a seller and a buyer, and one must always decide which one they want to be. But while in these moments, remember that it is easy to replace things, but hard to replace people.

    The people you will want to separate from, for they will be the enemies to your success; are Frank Fear, Tom Tomorrow, Joe Coffee, Charlie Chit-chat, and definitely Henny Penny (or Chicken Little if preferred). The only smart person to hang with would be Foxy Loxy.

It appears that the wisdom our farmer learned down on the farm was supplemented with some knowledge of chess. The basic principles of chess the farmer followed made the farmer a successful marketing entity. It was learned early in the game of chess that;

- One had to get off their dead apathy, and get to the scene of the action quickly, for mobility is everything.
- Next, control the center squares. Play to the center, or where pieces can bear down on the center. Control advisors and business environment.
- Reduce the pawn moves to a minimum. Rifle shoot, and do not shotgun the target market.
- Avoid winning unnecessary pawns. Know your priorities, and do not shoot from the hip.
- Play out the Queen early. Identify the other's problems, and wrong moves. Then scare the hell out of them, and turn their brain to jelly. Therefore, do not sell and forecast solutions first, but identify and sell the problem's first.
- Castling [w/ King]: Protect and move in a safe direction A.S.A.P. A basic client protection and diversification move.
- Never move same pieces time and again, and over and over. Use controlled power selling with clients by talking with them and not at them. Be receptive, observe and listen, and avoid sophistication while making the client feel important. The best marketing moves are to listen, watch, ask, and not talk.

Even though there is great farmer advice, and great chess moves directed for success; many business owners fail to achieve success, and remain stuck within a dormant status quo. The why so often is that they develop their own set of fairy tales, based upon ignorance and narrow mindedness; then get drawn into their own little fantasy world. These odd business owner management and marketing mythologies seem strange, and they are. It is as if they have cast spells upon themselves around the economic campfires of make believe, and then they start believing until it is true.

So don't get drawn into their fantasy world. These so-called business owners and marketing people live too much in their past. They become a legion in their own mind about events in their past; like that one great high school football game. Like once stated; "The farmer was out standing in his field," but years later everyone believed they said; "The farmer was outstanding in his field." There is an obvious difference, but in this world people are always looking for someone to tell them what they want to hear; - not what is right.

Note the five myths that keep many business and marketing people in the dark ages.

1. **"I don't need to change."** This is one sure way to become outdated and obsolete, and head towards a going out of business sale. Maybe even looking forward to an early poverty retirement.
2. **"My business, I built it, and if I want; I can sell it or close it?!?!"** Yeah, and then what are you planning to do for the rest of your life? This is maybe just some scare tactic to frighten his employees, or aggrandize his only fantasy of self importance within his own mind.
3. **"It's my money, and it's my business how I spend it."** This one is really a simplistic joke upon financial reality and tax law.
4. **"It is not so great to own your own business."** Now who is kidding who, and denying possible unemployability with equivalent income somewhere else. Plus, other employers might not like his personality. This goof-ball states all this while at an expensive resort with expensive dining, and sipping refreshing Singapore Slings and Piña Coladas.
5. **"My business is different."** No it isn't! This is a wives tale for fools trying to find an excuse for mediocre performance. Like it or

not, Federal, State and Local laws will treat him just like anyone else. Also, there is no type of a minor tax increase, or a minor new regulation that will put a winning person or successful business, out of business. They will just adjust, move forward, and conquer all.

It is alright for the above to have lots of opinionated opinions in their mind, but they should be wise enough to keep their mouth shut, and their opinions left to themselves. Then when at home, take a good look in the mirror, and note the ignorant person staring back at them.

So like it or not; if you're planning to be a successful business person, then you had better be a marketing person with learned people skills. Note that a commission salesman working as an independent contractor, or a manufacturers' representative on commission are both business owners. True they are self employed persons whose only real product is selling themselves first. Yet they also know there are certain tricks of the trade, that to some may seem irrelevant, but the tricks when followed improve the odds of controlling and closing the sale; whether the product is goods or services.

Therefore, please take note of the following simple list for controlled power selling techniques,' and for helping quadruple one's income to create wealth. Wealth like having the luxury of a nice 34' aft cabin power boat and/or a nice 34' Motor Home, and even a second vacation home at a nice resort area.

- Be sure your back is always to the "dead zone" when meeting with clients or potential clients. Since nothing will be occurring behind you that is more interesting than you. Pick a table in the restaurant where your back is to the wall or blind spot, then your guest will not be distracted by unrelated observable activities.
- Please have no tattoos showing, particularly on lower arms, the neck, or the hands. This one person could have been a great money making sales person, but he was a flop. Why? Because on one hand across the knuckles was written LOVE, and on the other HATE. Yet he was well educated, and one of the nicest guys you'd ever want to meet.

  The same goes for rings and jewelry in one's eyebrow, nose, and lips. This good rule even applies to huge dangling ear rings. Also, do not wear fancy diamond rings or a diamond watch, and do not drive up to a potential client's house or office with a fancy Porsche or Ferrari car.

- As a matter of fact, don't wear a watch period; for the moment you look or glance at it, the potential client gets turned off, and it is a little offensive. The client without saying a word to you, should they notice the glance, will think you have somewhere to go, or something more important to do at the time, - than be with them. Also, do not even have clocks around your office that clients will notice while you're making a presentation.
- Never smoke a good full hour or two before meeting with clients. The odor stays in the clothes, in your mouth, and in the car. This really offends and turns off non-smokers. Then you lose the sale, or fail to make your point. Also, (yeah it sounds dumb) make sure the finger nails are clean and cut, and the pinky finger nail is not one-half inch longer.
- Do you really want to relate and control people while in the office? Get rid of the big desk that sets between you and them. Purchase a nice big roll top desk, so that there is nothing big and restricting between you and the client. Just have a small wing table between you and them that, if needed, can be opened up for signature paper work.

  Of course it should be obvious; when meeting at a client's home, never sit in the living room on comfortable soft chairs. Direct everyone to sit at the kitchen or dining room table where you really have alert control and influence over the presentation. Also make the presentation visual with laid out bullet points, pictures and/or graphic illustrations. Now you're controlling more of their absorbing senses to react.
- Do not wear lapel pins and badges identifying connections or beliefs to associations, lodges, religion or political parties. Please stay neutral, and away from religion, politics, and social causes. Then if these marketing tricks are learned, one will become successful, and maybe even wealthy and rich.

  This confident professionalism will also provide one great freedom to politely say; "Stuff it!" For if one can successfully block and tackle where they are, then they can block and tackle anywhere else with the same confidence.

- Never, never say "Thank you!" The reason why is to avoid buyers remorse. Just congratulate clients on their decision to buy or act upon your guidance, for this reaffirms the client's actions to close the deal. One does not want the client subconsciously to later wonder; "Why is he thanking us?" Remember that the object of a top salesperson is to educate the client into buying a product or service, by showing future needs in order to sell them on present realities.
- Take note, and think about it. There are really only three great motivators to closing any deal with potential customers, or while trying to solicit and nail down new clients. The three great motivators are FEAR, IMITATION, and GREED. This is the area where one must learn to create graphic pictures in one's mind in order to direct their response.

  That is when a great marketing person can identify and sell the problems, and then the client buys the solution. Another way of putting it is to "scare the hell out of them, and turn their brain to jelly;" of course in a gentle kind way without them realizing your sales talent.
- Never, never and never exclude the spouse when practical and applicable to the business situation. Fact is, that the more connected spouses will make the sale for you; if they are treated as an equal with respect. Now if the situation is around family issues or involvement, always lean the presentation and educational information towards Mama.

  Never forget that only the Mama had the umbilical cord connection to the children, not the father who might be less concerned. So never forget that umbilical cords and breast feeding tend to slant opinions and objective viewpoints. The result occasionally is that the perfect solution is seldom the sellable solution.
- Quit using calling cards once you have become relatively established in the business. Develop a professional two or three fold slick color finished brochure. The brochure can be a one fold or two fold, and ends up at about 3 ¾ x 11 inches. Add to the brochure pictures or cartoon illustrations to emphasize key points. This subconsciously says to the prospective client, that you're not a beginner, not an amateur, and more likely a top professional in the field.

As often said, "It is not who you are, it is who you make people think you are." Therefore remember this; that in our free enterprise system, there are no real limitations, except self imposed limitations.

Again, this also means for one to be a winner and successful, someone else must lose, for second place has little value or recognition in marketing. The other place concept only has value in sports. The reality is, bronze and silver in business does not put food on the table, or pay the bills. Like that old saying; "A miss is as good as a mile."

Success matures with people skills once a person learns to analyze who that person is in front of them, or across the desk from them. Most certainly, any self motivated person would want to advance up the ladder from conscious incompetent, to unconscious competent, to conscious competent. The key is controlled communications by knowing who you're communicating with. So in a strange way, it's like the old saying of "Look before you leap."

The leading school of thought among winners and leaders in the fields of business and marketing is that people's personality types are divided into four major categories. Yet each category allows for, and recognizes, a good possibility for a slight blending with one of the other personality types. **So take note, and learn the following for success.**

Less Responsive

Analytical [*accurate*]	↔	**Drivers** [*efficient*]
↕		↕
Amiable [*agreeable*]	↔	**Expressive** [*stimulating*]

More Responsive

Of course, the left side with the analytical and amiable combination is less responsive, and the right side with the combination of the driver and expressive is definitely more responsive.

The driver alone is often easy to identify; for the driver tends to be very decisive, goal oriented, unorthodox, and only wants the bottom line issue and points of a presentation. Now several statements may describe the driver with more clarity: <u>One,</u> "The firings will continue until morale improves." Two, "Please be candid and tell me what is wrong with our operation, even if it means losing your job."

The driver often considers the firing of people to be a motivational seminar, for it gives fired employees an opportunity to have a turning point. A turning point to develop and improve one's employment history while working for a new employer. The driver refuses to live with a mistake; its fish or cut bait, get rid of window shoppers early, and then its sell or kill.

The driver/expressive has the same basic characteristic, but tends to be a little bit more compassionate with personality. They also tend to have the expressive ability to inspire enthusiasm, and display a broader talent for creativity. The expressive definitely displays better acquired people skills as if having an M.B.A. in leadership, rather then an M.B.A. in management.

Now the amiable is the one who loves to talk, visit, and too often be sociable to the point of frustration and boredom. This person tends to be too kind and polite. Yet the amiable often demonstrates stability under pressure, and tends to have an absence of pettiness in decision making processes.

Oh yes, the analytical; seldom exerts control or provides creative direction, and tends to be a fundamentalist inside the box thinkers. They are quite often weak with their communication skills, and tend to trap people into analysis paralysis. This most often is in the arena of accountants, actuaries, engineers, and chemists along with other paperwork book worms. That is why one should never ask an amiable/analytical; "What time is it?" Think about it!

Real business success depends upon one's ability to indentify another individual's personality traits early on. Then once identified, capitalize upon the situation by playing into the other persons identifiable traits listed previously in the four categories stated. This personality recognition for success is a learned skill that will develop into a true talent at controlled power selling, and this is what they call, "Success by Design."

Fact is, while early in one's career, it is natural to have stress when interacting with people, and for many it is insecurity for lack of experience that creates a state of flight (avoidance) vs. a state of fight (attack). This is why one must always leverage their talent upon other's experiences both good and bad. For being an advisor means to create and initiate a response, and not just wait, see, or react. This means having an emotional involvement with a client in a positive way, and not in a wishful way.

The learning experience takes a fast track once one learns that the art of communication is listening with the eyes as well as the ears, for it will seldom be your actions that will cause you to lose a client. The loss of a sale is usually first caused by your reaction, and the failure to identify the prospective clients reaction. A good people reader soon learns that about fifty-five percent of communications is non-verbal, as with body movements and facial reactions. With thirty-eight percent being tone of voice, and seven percent is semantics as to meanings and understanding of conveyed words to make one's point.

But let us not too quickly discount semantics. Example: What is the difference between ravaged and rapture? Answer: Salesmanship! This all means taking one's lack of prospective, and putting it into prospective. That is why top marketers are levelers of people with **PEP**; > **P**repare, **E**nthuse, **P**rime, and why they say that success only costs a **DIME**; > **D**esire, **I**nitiative, **M**ethod, and **E**ffort.

So in reality this explains why walking around in a fog is worse than having one's head up in the clouds. At least up in the clouds, one is learning how to operate outside of a vacuum, and not freeze up. So know that even diamonds in the rough have value, and most all diamonds have flaws such as lack of brilliance, feathers, and even internal black pepper spots not seen by the naked eye. These defects lock in the value, and the values cannot change or improve upon themselves.

Yet the beautiful thing with people is that they can improve upon their brilliance, get rid of their feathers and black spots, and add ever increasing value to their lives by prevailing over one's destiny. Being a professional means that no one has to supervise or manage you, for you instinctively have self direction, courage, and the commitment to prevail and succeed. Yet preceding all this, one needs to realize that they must first learn to understand themselves before trying to understand other people. Then take note as to how other people respond to your presence.

So as uniquely strange as this may sound, to be a successful business owner, marketing executive, or a managing boss, one must have:

- The Wisdom of Solomon.
- The patience of Jobe.

- The strength of Hercules.
- The skin of a rhinoceros.
- Plus; be a little bit crazy at times?!?! For tensions are one hell of a thing to try and relieve, and no one wants to drink a lot of Maalox.

There once was this frustrated and stressed out farmer, who always ended up paying so much extra over the basic price, every time he bought a new truck. Then one day the car dealer approached the farmer to buy a cow. The farmer decided to price the cow like this:

Basic cow - $250. Two-tone exterior - $45. Extra stomach - $75. Product storing department and dispersing service - $80. Four spigots ($10. each) - $40. Genuine cowhide upholstery - $145. Dual horns - $15. Automatic fly swatter - $35. Straw chopper and fertilizer attachment - $300. With total price, less the sales taxes - $985.

Now this really made the farmer feel good. The farmer never got mad or lost his cool, but he finally did get even with a nice personal feeling of satisfaction based upon his creativity.

This may be the appropriate time for a condensed version of a biblical story to thoroughly understand this business success game. One issue to understand within this game is the fact that there is never a second place. Like one getting a darn near blue ribbon for not making the sale or closing down the business deal. This biblical story is in the book of Ephesians, Chapters Five and Six. Here is where God makes it very clear that he never commands people to be successful, but only commands them to try. Then he promises them that if they go forward and try, he will make sure they are prepared to stand up and face the world with the proper gear. That gear being a whole suit of body armor necessary to move forward, and try for success. That being:

1. The loins will be girded to avoid injury.
2. Be given a solid breastplate for protection.
3. The feet will be shod with the best material.
4. Will be given the perfect shield for defense.
5. Provided a perfect helmet to save ones life.
6. Handed the perfectly forged sword, made by the best blacksmith.

So now everyone can go forth, and take on the world. Oop's! Not quite yet. Has it not been noticed that something is missing here? The warrior's backside is left unprotected. Guess this means we have to stand tall and face the world head on, and quickly learn how to cover our own ass. Yet be not depressed, for getting one's butt kicked early on is a learning experience. This is referred to as paying one's dues, and when one needs a mirror image self evaluation. The maturity factor here is learning from the butt kicking, and making sure it does not happen again; particularly if it involves the same set of circumstances and issues. That is why one has to appreciate that old saying; "Wound a king (the competition), and don't kill him, you become that darn near person in real trouble." The point is that YOU learned the lesson from the negative experience of failure, and went back to the drawing board to do the homework for being prepared for future encounters with success.

Now this is where one is developing the "Professional Edge," while maintaining a long selective memory to get even, and not lose again. So it might be that your competitors and negative opposition in the future may start referring to you as Doctor Doom. This will mean that you are now successful in your field, and well off with good fortune in this life. Then you will believe and think that living in the 'nasty now and now' is not so bad, and that it is definitely sweeter than the 'sweet bye and bye.' So when you start hitting the big ones, and pulling off the big clients that made one the big bucks; be modest, and learn from the undertakers' who know how to look sad at a $20,000.00 funeral.

Also, many envious people have said: "The price for success is that it is lonely at the top." This may be semi true, but one great benefit is that there is very little peer review or pressure at the top. Fact is that successful marketing people are just talented consultants who put a price tag on common sense. That is why one of the best training areas for marketing has one-hundred and forty years of solid history unimpeded by progress. They just keep adapting to the times, and keep racking in the big bucks with little outlying of expenses.

That industry is the life insurance industry with some of the best sales training with semantics in the world, and clear pat answer to objections. Fact is that a good insurance agent is really an investment banker, for they sell money. Then when the contract gets called to maturity, nothing provides a higher rate of return for the family or business. But objections must be met head on:

- We don't want that much life insurance. "Oh! Then you certainly do not plan on staying dead to long."

- We only want term. "Okay, but term is like wetting the bed. Sooner or later one must get up and do something about it, for term insurance may be great today, but it will be bad tomorrow."
- This is not the quoted premium, why should I pay for a rated policy? "Why? Because you will have less time to pay for it."
- "I am not applying pressure, for the pressure is already there; since we are working with your needs and objectives, - not mine."
- "The premium is not the problem, because the premium solves the problem." / "Your choice is big mistake vs. little mistake."
- Phrases and questions for repetitive use to create doubt, apprehension and insecurity for the prospective client/customer.

  "That's interesting! Why did you do it that way?"
  "I know I can help you."
  "I cannot keep the dogs from barking, but I can keep them from biting."
  "The other agent turned your beautiful asset into a creative liability, and that is now the big mistake that needs correction."
  "The cash shown is really a salvage value, not cash value. So the fact is that you win-win for the family, live, die, or become disabled."

- As for a business owner: "The policy protects the cash flow, and yet keeps value on the balance sheet; for it converts cash into cash value."
- "Term says that you do not plan on living past age sixty-five, and that you also do not plan on being successful."
- "Term insurance you buy, but with other types of contracts you rent, and when you're done using it, you get your money back (Salvage Value)."
- Do not argue if a person is term persistent. Just ask; "Okay! What kind of term do you want? One year, five year, ten year, twenty year, or for your whole life?" / "Okay! Whole life term it is."
- Now for the real death knell shot at current advisors when exposing their incompetency is to state: "I'm only giving you a basis to evaluate their professional abilities, - not your friendships."

Okay, some of these comments may sound a bit childish in content and ridiculously obvious. Yet they really work as a subliminal mind influencing form of directional control with pressure to close down the sale, or create the desired action to be taken in response. Also, most of these closing down statements with a little tweaking can be used by any marketing group or general business operation.

Note the following that was written on a huge black board before the start of a C.E.B.A. [Certified Estate and Business Analysts] conference:

W - - work > winner
O - - organization > operation
R - - repetition > referrals (Controlling the milk route.)
K - - knowledge > Karing (Serve first, keep your word.)

It is quite amazing to think that one can have all the brains, many degrees, and be in the best of health; but it is the interrelationships and communication skills with other human beings that most often decide the range of one's success. That is why this story about a little owl has relevance.

There was this little owl who would not hoot. The owl's mother was very worried, so she took him to a psychiatrist. The psychiatrist said to the little owl: "Now look; a dog barks, a cat meows, and a cow moos." The little owl quickly responded: "I know all that; I can hoot, and I have hooted; but when I do it scares the hell out of me."

So maybe the same thing happens when we hoot as beginners at real life, for hooting involves commitment, and quite often commitments will scare the hell out of us. Therefore, just as the owl must hoot, we as individuals must accept our hooting responsibilities. Believe it or not, once we get used to hooting, it is not so bad, and as a matter of fact feels pretty good.

So may "the driving force be with you!"

#

CHAPTER III

Financial and Economic common sense ideas to create wealth, and preserve success.

The academic fields of economics and finance have been made unnecessarily complicated for the vast majority of people. It's true that it apparently works well in the academic classroom, and for government economists. Yet, this arena has too often proved that one can be very intellectual, and also one-hundred percent ignorant at the same time. So as the old story goes; "Government economists have been one-hundred percent accurate in predicting four out of the last 18 recessions."

Therefore, this section might possibly have been better titled simply as "Think-o-nomics" or "Street Sense Economics and Finance" presented by participants, and not observers. The information will not have the statistical analytical void of reason, logic, or common sense that tends to hold individuals back from achieving success. For, like it or not, success in this area means taking risks, and overcoming one's fear, doubts and insecurity. Fact is, taking an action is a decision, but the reaction is a consequence. This conceptual view is sometimes referred to as the "Test of the Greater Fool Theory," with S.W.A.G.

To S.W.A.G. means that one must first obtain and review all the knowledge available at the time, and then stick their neck out by making a "scientific wild ass guess." The great General George Patton knew this principle well. So as the story goes; there was this top world renowned German Tank Commander and strategist General Rommel. General Rommel never lost a tank battle, and his Africa Corp. Tank Division was considered the best in the world.

Now there was this new American tank commander with inferior tanks as compared to the German's tanks, and he had to take on Rommel's superior Africa Corp. in the hot North African desert with mostly untested battle troops. At this point, General Patton and his troops were in a defensive position when Rommel's overwhelming force of troops and tanks started their attack on the American's defensive position. The result of the nasty, tough and bloody battle was that Patton and his now battle tested troops won the day, and Rommel's North African Tank Corp was soundly defeated and destroyed.

After winning the battle, General Patton loudly shouted out in front of his staff, where he was viewing the entire battle from his bunker position; - "Rommel, you magnificent bastard, I read your book."

This all proves that informational knowledge is a beautiful thing, and that one always improves their odds at winning with good beforehand common sense knowledge salvaged from other's experiences. In otherwards, a man's judgment is no better than his information. Fact is that all experts will be one-hundred percent right <u>and/or</u> one-hundred percent wrong eventually, and their authoritative claims of fact quite often become fiction. The fact is, as stated another way, most experts will be fifty-percent right half the time. This therefore might peak one's curiosity to wonder if astrologists might have a better track record at making economic and financial forecasts.

Now it is time to get down to ***the ten (10) ways to get rich, become wealthy,*** **or** ***just be successful with adequate financial security.***

But first, a comment about success, and one's perceptions of success. Success in life does not necessarily mean riches and wealth. It can be a state of being or frame of mind due to one's charitable or public service actions provided to society and the human race. The fact is that social class and wealth are not one and/or the same. Therefore, it is just a life decision as to whether one wants to operate as a non-profit being, or as a profitable being in our society. Yet as the old saying goes; "I have been rich and miserable, and I have been poor and miserable. Rich and miserable is better."

Okay!! Let's get back to the ten (10) ways to get rich.

[Some are tongue in check, but still factual.]

NUMBER ONE: <u>Inheritance.</u>

It is often quite beneficial to be the inheriting heir to family wealth provided by one's parents or grandparents. Yet sadly, and too often, family wealth is dissipated and blown away within six years of inheriting the family business or wealthy asset portfolio.

Like it or not, potential heirs just can't seem to get around the so-called negative local, state, and federal probate issues; Plus the dealings with lawyers, and the estate and inheritance taxes. So the best possible gift that a potential heir might provide to their future beneficial benefactor, may well be the forty-five page copy of the Federal #706 estate form. Needless to say that this #706 form may help to protect and preserve one's future interest if previewed in advance.

The sad part is that the majority of heirs that inherit wealth have a complete ignorance and unawareness of reality when it comes to handling their good fortune. The majority are just rich, but not successful, and could not find or fight their way out of a paper bag. Also, many have been led down the "primrose path" with new friends and acquaintances. So this is why some wise man once said; "All fairy tales have an ending, and occasionally the dragon wins."

So it is never really a question of how much you earn or inherit, but how much you keep when all the vultures within the system want access to your money and your wealth. So as the old story goes; "Wise bankers never die, they just yield to maturity." But you and your future benefactors should remember this, that "Shrouds do not have pockets."

NUMBER TWO: Marriage.

There once upon a time was this woman, who as a professional motivational speaker, went around the country holding seminars for young women. The seminars were to educate young women on how to marry right, and capture the rich successful male; even if it meant taking the male from someone else. This speaker always forgot to mention the fact, that if you marry for money, you will end up earning every damn dime of it sooner or later.

But this speaker wisely pointed out, that one should make sure that the new successful spouse is at least fifteen to twenty years older than themselves; the older the better. Now it surely does not take an actuary to figure this one out as a developing source of wealth, while enjoying a higher standard of living; but it may seem that these comments are a little lopsided. So to balance it out, the fact is that there are many, many men looking for older women as a "nurse and a purse," for this is particularly true with men over age 59 ½. This senior citizen arena is an easy target area for men, for there are about seven single older women widows and divorcees for each still living and dancing male; with or without Viagra.

Just imagine the opportunities with some of these rich widows whose wealthy successful husbands died first with large pension funds and insurance policies. So at this point, a few wise sayings may prove valuable and appropriate; like. . . "Pearls melt in vinegar." / "The Glass Slipper may become a combat boot." / "The silk purse may revert back into the sow's ear." / "Caution about that free cheese in the mouse trap."/ "There is no fool like an old fool (particularly when they get lonely, and their lifetime care giver spouse prematurely disappears.)" / Now the Rocky Horror Picture Show comment becomes relevant; "You're spaced out on sensation, like you're under sedation."

This area of wealth acquisition is a two-edged sword. So, "we must always keep ourselves awake, and not allow ourselves to fall asleep mentally." Then as mentioned early on, the much younger spouse may eventually earn every damn dime of it before the actuarial statistics bear themselves out. As when the crew points out on a vacationing cruise ship, that younger spouse who now has extra baggage. Particularly that baggage they are pushing around in a wheelchair or assisting with a walker while having that oxygen tank tube up the nose. **Oop's!!** - Cannot walk away now. They're too close to winning the jackpot, and getting the golden egg from the golden goose. So they now must just grin and bear it, for they're now earning it.

NUMBER THREE: Win the Lottery.

Proves that the one in ten or twenty million occasionally beat the odds. This has actually been the new number one millionaire wealth creator in the United States for many a year. Just think about it; for just about every week, and certainly every month, someone or a group is winning a lottery with huge dollar amounts. Yet many also get conned out of their money, or spend it foolishly and wastefully while still alive. While others somehow get raped, pillaged and plundered when they die by unethical lawyers, accountants, and investment advisors; but that's life.

These lucky souls should learn that the single most important word for them to use without feeling bad is, - "NO!" Then the next important two words that they learn should be, - "No Way!" These two responsive answers to their friends, relatives and strangers are a must; even if it makes one feel as if they're "the only tree in the dog pound."

Now the best place to go first for trusted, neutral, independent, and honest guidance and advice is a nationally recognized Bank Trust Company. Never, never first go to an investment advisor or counselor, an independent lawyer or law firm, and certainly not to a local accountant or enrolled tax agent. If you do, you're just asking to have it stuck to you while living, or to your heirs while dying later. Take this fact to the bank: Many single elderly rich lottery winners have been money laundered by their estate lawyer, and their so-called trusted accountant for millions of unearned dollars upon and after their death.

Enough said on this topic.

NUMBER FOUR: Crime/White collar { A sad fact of reality is that economics and finance too often have a dark side }:

This is one area about getting rich in this life, which has a clear double standard as to ethical accountabilities and responsibilities for business executives and politicians. Next, would be the failure among the major WASP,H. business schools to adequately teach proper ethics, integrity factors, and social responsibility issues to their graduates. Plus, spend less time in class on how to create "Chainsaw" employment and management contracts to rip off public and charitable corporations.

The ones that teach naïve and impressionable students how to go right up to the razor's edge; without crossing the line of legality, but ethics is a different issue. Then how as executives, they can push the envelope with techniques on how to cook the books, and inflate stock values. Also, let us not forget, the valuable educational part about how to control and manipulate the Board of Directors.

Is it not interesting that a top executive officer within a company can be fired, or forced to resign, for any number of nefarious reasons, and they still get big multi-million dollar separation bonuses. Maybe one should consider sending their children to a major WASP,H. business school for learning quietly and with subtlety to become an incompetent, unethical, or conniving crooked C.E.O.? Wow!! Then get $34,-millon just to get fired, or One Point Three Billion for bad ethical health within a unified health caring environment.

So who then would care if their resume looks bad, now that they are considered unemployable, and cannot possibly get another job? A reasonable person might think that $34,-million or more, might make one and his family financially secure for life, and that they could all sleep well throughout the night. This moment in life is called "Psychic Income or Peace of Mind."

It should be, but it is not quite clear, about the government's oversight status and involvement with big business. Yet there is definitely no room at the inn here for the government pot to be calling the business kettle black. Should one think otherwise, do the research concerning what happens at the direction of our government when anyone interferes with U.S. business interest, and uses the word nationalization? This was, and is all protected with "Trompi L'oell," and the game's principle objective is to "Create Fog." In other words, create an alternate reality in the public's mind for deception.

It may be amazing and shocking for some to know that many democratically elected leaders have been suddenly ousted from power, and dispatched into oblivion for the benefit of our U.S. energy, mineral and agricultural business interest; even for sewing machines. Therefore, it is just too bad that some famous names like Mossadegh, Allende, Durante, Arellano, Diem, Balaquer, Garcio, <u>Colby</u>, <u>Helms</u>, and the 'King of Deception' with the <u>Forty-Committee</u> are not available at this moment for inquiry verification.

This section will endorse the recommended reading of several books, and a quote from Gloucester; "As flies to wanton boys', are we to the God's; they kill us for their sport." So one's desire for non-fictional knowledge should have you read the following: > "The Predator's Ball" - by Connie Bruck / "Serpent on the Rock" / A series of three books; - "Shadows, Skulls and Spooks *<u>I</u>*, ***<u>II</u>***, & *<u>III</u>*." / And finally, "The Age of the Great Depreciation."

NUMBER FIVE: <u>Talent</u>.

Well what can one say? The fact is that 99.999% is learned, developed and improved upon by experience. So we all can't sing like a talented ten year old opera singer, or as a home care maker from Scotland. Nor be one who has the naturally developed and instinctive eye hand coordination with intelligence to be a top vascular surgeon, neurosurgeon, oral surgeon, or a highly trained radiation-oncologist. Fact is, even the majority of those in the medical field could never advance forward into these types of specialty skills.

Therefore, to be talented one must learn to put last things first, so that one will know where they are really going in life. Then along with that, remember that it is never nice to try and fool Mother Nature, and that talented people are never, never Lemmings.

A talented person in economics and finance needs to be cognizant of the reality as stated in Rocky Horror Picture Show; "One can remove the cause, but not the symptoms." Therefore it is important to recognize and appreciate the Chinese word for CRISIS. This word is made up of two symbols; the first part an idiographic meaning "danger," and the second part being an ideogram meaning "opportunity." The point is, believe it of not; that it takes real talent to avoid one, and capitalize upon the other.

So this must mean that one should understand the "Law of Probable Disbursement," and recognize the true meaning of ***being an expert.*** With "Ex" -> meaning 'has been,' and "pert" -> a drip under pressure. Oh! And yes; the law of ... > "When the crap hits the fan, it is never distributed equally."

Now for a nice story about a real jerk. This angry attorney in a client meeting stated to prove his credibility; "I've been a practicing attorney for over twenty years." Wow! What can one say? Oh yes! This lawyer has been practicing for over twenty years, and shows he has not gotten it right yet; he must still be practicing?!?!

Now two stories about two different and talented individuals whose eye catching gimmick billboards received a lot of attention. Both ideas paid off big time. Billboard one: *"You can now borrow all the money you need to get completely out of debt."* Billboard two: *"Life's too short, get a divorce."* Tactful? Maybe not; but profitable.

So in closing, real talent quite often means thinking outside the box, not appearing overly educated, and not over thinking situations in life. The following story may illustrate these points: There were three college graduates at a job interview; one from Harvard, another from Princeton, and one from Akron University. The human resources manager had to screen one out for the job. So he put all three in the room and asked one question; "How many seconds are there in the year?" The Harvard person said; "About two and a half million plus or minus." The Princeton guy stated: "That is much too complicated to know and calculate at this moment."

Now the Akron University nobody stated that he knew the exact answer. Then the Harvard and Princeton applicants in unison said, "No Way!!" The Akron boy said; "Yes way!! - The answer is twelve" The other two laughed and said; "You're nuts! The Akron boy said; "Maybe, but the answer is still twelve. Like you know January 2nd, February 2nd, March 2nd, April 2nd, and so on and so on it goes."

So who might you as the human resource person have hired?

NUMBER SIX: Invention.

Many, let's say quite a few, multi-million dollar inventors had little or no formal education. Yet early on, they had unrecognized genius while in grades K thru 12. So undoubtedly through their genes they must have inherited the necessary insight, logic and wisdom to invent something of value. Unfortunately for most of these wealthy inventors, they quite often lacked the necessary and adequate people skills to market themselves, or manage a business operation. But fortunately, often by accident, they surrounded themselves with savvy marketing people; be they a lawyer, accountant, or a shrewd business management person. But sadly many get ripped off early on, and never get to experience the multi-million dollar success club.

Nearly all of these deep thinking and creative individuals were very nice people, but often quite introverted while being a little eccentric. Several noted exceptions have been practicing professional medical people who invented orthopedic devices, and non-carcinogenic inter-body adhesives. Yet there were a few creative individuals that had the personality of a rattle snake. Where the employees and advisors needed to cover their rear-ends, and tread with caution when working with their often temperamental talents. So when working in this rather reclusive arena, there is often the rare situation that adds new meaning to the economic formula of "Risk Tolerance vs. Benefit Rewards," or as Alexander Pope said; "Fools rush in where angels fear to tread."

But the fact remains, that these individuals stuck their neck out, took the risk of being eaten alive by "Social Darwinism;" and still beat the dragon. So had these rare creative individuals not done so with their unknown inventions of value, and had they not surrounded themselves with smarter and wiser men than themselves; they'd most likely be poor mediocre so and so's living off entitlement programs. Instead, most enjoy a nice life, with nice assets, and often like to think of themselves as Las Vegas or Atlantic City whales.

There were many times when socializing around these successful people, that one would think the stork had an accident; an unexpected accident while flying them towards their delivery. An unintentional accident when the delivery stork dropped the babies upon their heads before the actual delivery. Then another thought too often enters the mind by Ralph Waldo Emerson; "There are many things for which a wise man may wish to be ignorant." The why was that way too many of these individuals clearly proved that social class and wealth are not the same. Enough said!!

NUMBER SEVEN: Investments:

This has always been a favorite arena for eating people alive, and cannibalizing upon people's ignorance, greed, and being too analytically educated beyond their intelligence. Yet be aware, this is not one of the "K.I.S.S." areas meaning "Keep it simple stupid.' 'K.I.S.S. in this section means Knowledge, Initiative, Study, and Simplicity." So let's start off early with small bullet points with bits and pieces of simplicity. The why is, that in this section, we are dealing with micro real world economics and finance.

- Readers don't buy, and buyers don't read. That just proves that a little knowledge will get one into deep doo-doo, and into dangerous waters. So always do your homework.
- No one ever bought a bad investment; it just turned out that way. Since any golfer knows that Sand Happens!
- Any dead fish can swim down stream.
- One never gets hurt jumping out of a basement window.
- Never a high risk tolerance when people lose money; plus they suddenly have "Short memories" and "Selective memories."
- Never invest in anything that eats while you sleep; unless you just happen to be a successful farmer. Think about it?!?!
- Any blind person can walk down a straight hallway.
- The meek may inherit the earth, but not the mineral rights.

Real Estate: The fantasy world of get rich quick guru's, who hold seminars, write books, and rip everyone off with learning fees. Yet the proof is in the pudding, when over time, most of them ended up in bankruptcy, went to jail, left the country, or became termite specialist. So remember this;

- God is only in the real estate business, not into stocks and bonds.
- Ah yes! People too often forget that the real estate business is an art form. So they then create real problems by trying to make it into a science.
- Remember that those who live by the sword will die by the sword. Sorry, meant to say "Live by leverage, will die by leverage."
- Real Estate investors often forget R.O.A. > "Return on aggravation." This being one of the most overlooked profit margin factor.
- Oop's! > Compared to a bad tenant; a vacancy is an absolute delight.
- People like income all the time, for it is socially acceptable.
- Never follow the sheep or chase the herd, and that includes idiot lemmings. Therefore, avoid group think.
- Don't fish in the sewer, or be a bottom fisher. Would you buy an ugly ill fitting suit because it is cheap?
- Stop! Look! Listen! > For they who "panic first, panic best." Then the question becomes; "Where is the blood? Once that answer is found, it is time for the vultures to do vulturine flights.
- Safe/Guaranteed! **Okay**! Guaranteed by who?
- Never lost a-*(current)*-client's money. True? The ones that lost money, just are no longer their clients.

Investor: Never fall in love with an investment, and if it sounds too good to be true; it usually is.

- Never buy into a rising hot market (any market), for markets sway and operate upon 100% greed, and/or 100% fear. So the whole realm is pure mental perceptions vs. emotional reactions.
- With stocks, one only buys the lows, and rents the highs. That is why the hard part is not the knowing when to buy, but the trick or art of the business is knowing when to sell.
- The only thing predictable about the stock market, is its unpredictability. Therefore, "you must remember that; -

- Pigs get fat, hogs get slaughtered. Bulls' party, brag, spend like fools, and then commit suicide. While bears wish they would have, and often have second thoughts, but they tend to sleep well after reading all of the negative news.
- As the old saying goes; "One must decide whether they want to eat well or sleep well."
- One must learn to depend upon property at work, and not just themselves at work, because the "future is no longer what it used to be." Here is where everyone begins too fall into the category of economic aging, and finances tend to become more critical. True, from 50 to 60 you're still on the "Go-Go TRACK!" At age 65 to 70 in good health, often starts the state of "GO-SLOW!" Age 75 plus and still fairly independent in a state of "SLOW-GO!" Now over age 75, range of age to 85 often known as "NO-GO!" Many times with dependency care issues, and with cash flow now having even greater value.
- Mister J.C. Penny may have given everyone a clue for success when he said; "Buy straw hats in January."
- Crisis investing is in tangibles like gold, silver, and platinum; - for gold and other valuable commodities are an indicator of monetary error. This usually occurs when investors suddenly learn that they invested in Extremely Limited Partnerships, Great Sinking Debentures, and that their penny stocks weren't worth a nickel.

Retirement requires planning in advance, because...

- Retirement is unemployment, and dependent means broke.
- T'is not a question of dollars wanted at age 65, but what the purchasing power of those dollars will be after age 65.
- One must preserve their "choices" so they can decide when and how to retire.
- Everything cycles, but inflation and taxes are a constant. So the fact is that one's capital needs never go down.
- One should note that inflation is cumulative, and that inflation creates a loss of, or erosion of one's purchasing power. This is referred to as the "time value of money."
- The above is why the successful person plans for generations, and the poor (Sorry, financially impaired.) plan for Saturday night.

- Question? Which one do you think your financial advisor is more concerned about? > Your retirement or their retirement?
- Thinking Halloween is scary? Try starting your retirement savings after age 50?!?! Good Luck!
- Retirement planning means **C.P.R.** > **C.** - create $'s, **P.** - preserve your $'s, **and R.** - restore lost $'s. For here is where time is both your ally and your enemy.

Based upon the previous points; it may always be best to be a contrarian, and never allow yourself to be sold on emotion and the excitement of the moment. The reality is, one needs informational facts, and lead time to think and reason things out. To do otherwise will brand you with the unwanted title of either "**Elephant** (Person with a trunk full of money)," "**Quaker** (Person naïve enough to pay full price)", "**Fish** (Dumb sucker who believes everything, does not do their homework, and it hurts their feelings to say NO!), "**A Whale** (Person loaded with a lot of lard, ready to be turned into oil, and dumb enough to beach themselves. These dim-wits do not even have to be harpooned.)."

Therefore, there are really only four barriers to wealth accumulation. **One** is Taxes, **two** is Inflation, **three** is Probate, **and four** is SELF! So to start with, one must learn how to avoid paying their taxes, while not evading their taxes. The objective being quite clear is to only pay your fair share, and not your full share. Since taxes affect one's net cash flow to the negative, one must consistently plan for lower taxes. The key is first to convert present ordinary income into future capital gains. Second, create present tax free compounded growth. Third, create present non-recapturing tax free income. So please note that one plans for lower taxes to create and maintain cash flow, cash flow, and cash flow. Next is to design a well thought out plan to convert tax dollars into assets, and at the same time create the tax free transfer of taxable wealth.

This legal tax avoidance, manipulation and conversions game is where one needs, and must have, a very 'competent' accountant, or C.E.B.A. advisor. Here though is the problem; most accountants do not do income tax planning, they only do income tax calculating. They are more often concerned about the current year's bottom line, than with financial long range implications. This should be of no surprise, for the majority of accountants are only the historians of the record. They are being mostly the rear view mirror calculators of only current and past performance. So a creative, competent, thinking out of the box accountant is worth every dollar and dime that they earn.

Therefore, to improve one's odds and performance in the market, one needs to know that "BOND investing is a science, and that STOCK investing is a calculated risk." **So with bonds...**

- The key is to always know the NAV [Net Asset Value], and it's best to buy the bonds or bond funds on the secondary market at a price below NAV.
- The key then is to know their rating: AAA, AA, A, BBB, BB, B, Etc., or no rating. Note that the best bonds 'Earn' their ratings rather than 'Buy' (Insured) their ratings.
- So with bonds one needs to know the Coupon, Maturity, Calls, Price, Rating, Yield, and the Quality. As they say with bonds, "don't take a bite until you know what is inside."
- Example: AA/Revenue Bond/20 years/4.5%/Calls after 5 years. Also be aware if buying at par or at a premium, for this affects yield.
- Note that after you purchase a bond; should interest rates go up, the bond face value goes down (this could cause you a liquidity loss if you needed your funds.). Now if interest rates go down, the bond value increases, and you have a Capital Gain; - Not Bad!

Now as for stocks, the starting point is often reviewing over the trunk rear-view mirror statistical observations. But naïve analytical observer souls think that everything that can possibly be known about the market is already built into the stock price. These naive classroom observers known as PhD's refer to this as the Efficient Market Theory; an investment theory about a provable rational market that is endorsed by academic nerds. Don't think so, if one was ever an active participant investor dealing with their own money.

Historical specific performance information is misinformation. There is nothing useful shown about the future, and too often the current prologue superior performance record tends not to persist. But should one be analytically inclined and curious, go for it with the following.

- Price to Book - - 1 to 1 ½ okay. 2 ½ is high, 3++ not so good.
- Price to Earnings - - average is 18 times, 28 times looking bad.

- Then go deeper with Price to Sales, Long Term Debt vs. Total Capital, Dividend Yields, Price Earnings to Growth [Project 3 to 5 years EPS]:
- Then good show-off talking points are; - ALPHA > Ability to value fluxations as Plus/Even/Minus; - BETA > Constant with #1 as base, as with the S&P 500 or 100; - STANDARD DEVIATION > the measure of volatility [the plus or minus off the mean returns]. Oh! The Sharpe ratio?
- **Yet,** it all boils down to whether you end up "Buying or Selling too late **vs.** Buying or Selling too soon; which will it be?

STOP!! STOP!! - Even if one does all this stuff, it is still S.W.A.G.

But first some more market analyst slush terms to be amused by, which seems to keep everyone dependent upon their analytical opinions:

- IRR - "Internal Rates of Return."
- ERR - "Effective Rates of Return."
- PVD - "Present Value Discount."
- TWR - "Time Weighed Returns."
- EPS - "Earnings Per Share (With 3 to 5 year projections.)."
- ROE - "Return on Equity."
- Regression lines compared to Capital Market lines
- "Call"> a buy/bet the stock will rise; "Put"> a buy/bet the stock will fall. A Put is buying cheap insurance to protect one's downside losses.
- Now one needs to note: "Price Earning to Growth"/ "Price to Sales" / "Long Term Debt *vs*. Total Capital"/ "Dividend yield payout ratio as a percentage of earnings."

Wow!! Was this not a lot of goodie-goodie valuable information that everyone just needs, and must know to be successful? Don't think so! So just wait until understanding the principal theory of 25/75 in the tomorrow is today.

Simplicity is, just go out and invest in a professionally managed, renowned well known "NO-Load" Mutual Fund or ETF; be it in Bonds, Stocks, Commodities, or a Government Securities Fund. **Caution:** Think twice before doing the same and/or similar investment with "Tax-deferred" annuities of any type. Do the research into their hidden and so-called non-existent commissions. The discovery clue is the "bail-out" provisions; that's the penalty withheld should you ask for or need your money back within an established time period. Also, be aware of a possible "MVA" clause, known as a Market Value Adjustment clause [This can get one killed.]. It simply means the annuity company does not have to keep its word or promise. **Also,** compare the annuity's high annual internal insurance fees of 2 ½% plus/minus to that of a no-load mutual fund's fees of .65% plus/minus.

Now assume that both a similar mutual fund **vs.** a similar annuity have identical appreciation results; - unlikely! With the annuity you automatically lose. Why? The annuity gain is taxed as ordinary income. Then God forbid if one should die; the annuity gets no "Step-up-in basis [Date of Death Valuation], then all gains are taxed as ordinary income. **Final point:** Never put a tax shelter in a Tax Shelter; but even then, the annuity has that nasty age 59 ½ penalty rule.

Oh!! Least one forgets; never annuitize an annuity or anything else. The insurance company annuitizing is like a casino, for the house always wins. You see, the insurance company has a better actuary calculating when you might die, than you have risking your savings on how long you might live. That is why one must always do their DUE DILIGENCE, with valid, equal, and fair comparisons.

NUMBER EIGHT: ***Longevity.***

What can one say? If you "live long and prosper," you may have it made in the shade; but if you outlive your money, your ass is grass. So the person with longevity had better learn about the Rule of Seventy-two early in life. This simple rule tells one at what interest rate it takes, and the years needed for one's money to double. Now for several examples: You have $1,000.00 earning 5%. Now divide 5% into 72, and it will take 14.4 years for one's money to double. At 10% > 7.2 years, and at 3% > 24 years. With these factoring results, one had best start saving early.

Now here are some numbers with one making the same regular annual contribution, or with only one date certain annual lump sum deposit. All this regularity needed to have **One-Million dollars available at age 65.** Both calculated at a 12% annual rate of return on the investment. But if only achieved a 6% return, will need to double the amount shown, or cut the benefits at 65 in half.

- Age 25: > Monthly $84.00 / **or** Lump sum - $10,747.00 once.
- Age 35: > Monthly $283.00 / **or** Lump sum - $33,378.00 once.
- Age 45: > Monthly $1,001.00 / **or** Lump sum - $103,667.00 once.
- Age 55: > Monthly $4,304.00 / **or** Lump sum - $321,974.00 once.

So getting rich is simple, right? Just invest well, and don't lose money.

Oop's!! - Now the deep question becomes, how long will one's money last? Not even factoring in the effects of inflation as to the time value of money, and loss of purchasing power. The following will be calculated at a **5.5%** annual rate of return, while making regular monthly withdrawals against the accumulated savings amount, and the interest. Age here is not an issue.

- **$250.000.00** > $2,673.00 monthly for 10 years; *for* 20 years $1,686.00 per month, and forever if withdrawing interest only $1,108.00 per month.
- **$750,000.00** > $8,025.00 monthly for 10 years; *for* 20 years $5,055.00 per month, and forever if withdrawing interest only $3.330.00 per month.

This is certainly enough information to make the point. Now this only reminds me of that old saying; "Most people want to arrive, they just do not want to take the trip." So maybe it's time for some humor.

- "Creativity is moving the books on how to get rich in real estate from the Business Section of the library, into the Humor section."
- "Who would have thought, one would live long enough to see the day when you would write a perfectly good check, but the bank would bounce."
- "The only problem with living to be a hundred; it is so time consuming."
- "Retirement is when you get socks, underwear and earmuffs for Christmas, - and you're glad."

NUMBER NINE: **<u>Entrepreneurship</u> [A great way to go.].**

All that really needs to be said is; if you have the talent, drive, ambition, and the courage to be a risk taker, go for it! **Note** that if you're afraid of failing and stumbling, forget it! But take note, this is one of the best ways to become rich and successful, along with creating future wealth. So all that you will need to do is take the risk, and be a contrarian. Then seek knowledge, work your ass off, and follow the basic rules of the road with integrity; all while dealing with employees and one's future customers and clients. This is often referred to as the "Serve First" principle.

The next realm of attainment is to seek out 'competent advice,' that is given only by 'competent' legal or accounting advisors. This will be a tough job to accomplish, for a college degree, business certifications, or a big name is not the "Good Housekeeping Seal of Approval."

So when starting your business, just operate as a Schedule C - Sole Proprietor until you start making some real money, but if liability is an issue by the nature of the business; then and only then become an S-Corp. or L.L.C. Both of these types of corporations are known as pass through income entities, where all of one's income and profits are taxed at one's personal tax bracket on a calendar year basis. Therefore, one's business is only a corporation in name only, with no special cash flow benefits, but it does allow one to keep their expenses and losses on their personal tax return.

Yes, there may be some exception dealing with valid limited liability issues around products and services, or with professional partnership liability exposure for the wrongful acts of the other partners. This is fine as long as you are not yet successful and profitable, or as a medical or dental professional corporation. Once you become successful with adequate personal income to live on, and adequate income for operating the business; -> get the hell out of the S or LLC Corporation. Immediately make the election with IRS to become a C-Corp. with a Fiscal Year, and then accounting wise, close down the books at the elected fiscal year date on the S or LLC.

Now should you hear this from the accountant or lawyer; "You do not want to be an 1120 C-Corp. for you will then have to pay a double tax." - Fire them, and run quickly to a new accountant or lawyer that is a '<u>competent</u>'

advisor. One should know that an 1120 C-Corp. pays a much lower tax on the earned excess profits, has way better fringe benefit advantages, and then the two separate and different tax returns do not become due on the same date; so farewell to the kiss of death on cash flow benefits and profits.

Fact is, only you own yourself, and you own your C-Corp. Then I do not think you will cheat yourself. So pay a lower tax on profits, and be your own banker within the C-Corporation. Then capitalize upon the dividend exclusion allowance to invest the cash reserves, and create proper excess accumulation wealth within your own internal bank at lower tax rates. Better yet, create tax-free cash flow without recapture. Wow! Only with an 1120 C-corporation.

So as they say; "It is as you wish it." Therefore, remember a 'competent' advisor's job is to guide his client, and help reposition his client's assets to: **One:** Pay less taxes to improve cash flow. **Two:** Create more income potential. **Three**: Develop more wealth. **Four:** Reduce the headaches and complications of probate; without unnecessary cost, or any potential loss of wealth. **Five:** Create asset protection from all types of potential liabilities.

Again, go for it! You will have no need for a pink rabbit's foot.

NUMBER TEN: None of the above.

Okay, with all now said and done; this is in reality the nasty now and now about living today. Therefore, it is understandable that you only want to be comfortable, have peace of mind, a sense of security, and not have to worry about the sweet bye and bye down the road. Well, best of luck to you.

The only semi-safe suggestion here to obtain this objective is to become a public service employee with the Federal or a State government. Yes, there are also a few big city and big county government opportunities. Of course, a good military retirement is nice for one, as long as they don't get killed, or badly and dependently disabled for life. Please note that economics does not really mean that much when you're nipples down for life.

Let's be honest and admit that public service may not be so bad. For after all, a lot of public servants doing the same identical job as many others out in the non-government civilian world, will make 30% to 40% more in pocket payroll income. Now in addition to this, they have far better living and retirement benefits on everyone else's tax dollars. This so-called security blanket of entitlement, as it exists today, was clearly not so desired or beneficial in the prologue past. Back when, in the prologue past, it was where the unemployables got employment. Need one say more?

So in closing out this chapter; remember that 'Sand Happens' without knowledge, but it also happens with knowledge. So as the Boy Scout Motto states; -"Be Prepared." For the whole reality game is simply to improve one's odds at achieving success early on in one's life.

#

CHAPTER IV

Government, $-nomics, Politicians
* YOUR MONEY *
[Eunuchs, Donitz, Observers, and Pipers.]

This stated arena for prevailing over obstacles and interlopers requires a lot of mature wisdom, and a lot of continuing education to achieve and maintain one's financial success. A line from Windows on the World may help make the point; "The trouble with the future is, it is no longer what it used to be." And yes, as previously stated; "never play in another man's ball game." But! This is one of those 'however' exceptions, since the government has made itself the referee, and also the opponent player within the same game.

I do not want to bust anyone's bubble, but naive thinking when it comes to our government can block one's success like "a thief in the night." Yet, the government blessing is that they pass overly worded and comprehensively vacuumed laws, rules, and poorly thought-out regulations. So the intent should be to read their refereeing book, and beat them at their own game; even at the point of taking away their so-called home field advantage.

The beauty of all this is that the rules were passed by a committee, and our congress is just a big oversized committee. For them to succeed, they must operate to the lowest common denominator by compromise. Now WOW! Why WOW? Because, this provides beautiful gaps in thought and meaningful interpretations called 'Loopholes.' Here is where professional advisors find the blind spots, and put the regulator's hand into their own bear trap.

A good advisor regularly reads his government training manual, finds the gap in government thinking, and knows how to make the government fall upon its own sword, without his client hopefully becoming a test case. The following may make the point as to a top advisor's worth.

Note the price list for answers;

- A general answer, - - - .75 cents
- Answer requiring thought, - - - $1.25
- The correct answer, - - - $2.15
- Please note that dumb looks are still, - - - FREE.

This is why hiring a competent profession advisor who knows the trade is worth every dime paid to them. They will follow the referee's rules when pushing the envelope, and while only going up to the razor's edge. But beware of, and learn too avoid, the miracle witch doctors on the constitution, Houdini tricksters on tax evasion, along with the Moe Joe ex-government employee connections. Sad truth is that there are many ex-F.B.I. agents, ex-I.R.S. personnel and ex-government attorneys who have been sent to jail for ripping off the naïve public with get rich quick schemes, or tax evasion schemes.

Please note; "Render unto Caesar that which is Caesar's," and only short change Caesar by using his own verifiable rules with loopholes against him. For should one decide otherwise, then play the game of "Monopoly," pass Go, and Go to Jail. So note, that for every exit there is an entrance somewhere else, and for every entrance this is a - Oop's! Is not hindsight with 20/20 vision, along with short and selective memories just wonderful?

Yes! Everyone loves, and should love our American history, the founding fathers, the Bill of Rights, and the Constitution. The admiration is yesterday, but one must live in the realities of today. The today with new "Geo-political" economics, "Geo-political" multi-national corporations, and the third world realities of "BRICE." Now we add into the mix our modern day Congress with the issues they must face, domestic and foreign, for the sole purpose of preserving our American values for future generations.

But the truth is that business economics and government economics make strange bedfellows, and they are always testing out the "Greater Fool Theory." So here's one thought to think about; always be careful who gives you a helping hand? They may not be an Uncle Bill with a helping hand, but just the wrong hand out to the contrary benefit. As a business owner desiring success you must be profit oriented, and only think cash flow profits. Not like the government, for they prefer debt to profit in trying to accomplish their objectives.

Now let us first lighten up a bit with many assorted and satirical words of wisdom. Wisdom expounded by numerous enlightened individuals with great insight into our government and Congress.

- "Political speeches are a lot like buying a car; - infinite promises and limited warranties."
- "One was in shock when they entered the lobbyist restroom at the Capitol building, for above each urinal was a sign stating; "Please do not eat the mints."
- "Trusting a politician to balance the budget is the nearest thing I know to asking a 'Samurai' to do your vasectomy."
- "Congress can't make death any worse, but they can make the act of surviving terrible."
- *As they say;* "Washington gives, and Washington takes away, because it is the dealer, and we are not allowed to cut the cards."
- *Remember;* "Government regulations are designed to prevent capitalism between consenting adults."
- "Government always seems to put a cost on productive behavior, and gives incentives for unproductive behavior." Or to put it another way; "Entitlements reward the unproductive, and penalizes the productive."
- As the good Margaret Thatcher put it; "Socialism works well until the people paying for it run out of money." She indirectly hit the nail on the head; for socialism's entitlements, like it or not, too often destroys initiative and the incentives to move forward and succeed.
- "Preachers and Politicians do their best work when your eyes are closed. That's why I've always been afraid of politicians and dogs. I don't know why, for I have never been bitten by a dog."
- "Deficits are the governments' way of saying Oop's! Yet what make the deficit even more interesting is that they did it while buying from the lowest bidder."

- "No question about it; if the government had to operate like a private business, they'd have had a fire along time ago."
- "If Patrick Henry thought taxation without representation was bad, - he ought to see it with representation. Could be that taxation without representation might have been cheaper?"
- 'Somehow it doesn't seem fair that Fantasy Island was cancelled, but Congress goes on and gets renewed."
- "For the Democrats; the show 'Lifestyles of the Rich and Famous' is escapist entertainment, but for the Republicans it is a training film."
- "When taking a good look at Congress, one clearly notes that the budget is not the only thing that is unbalanced."
- "Everything is relative; for a senator or representative it is taking a summer break. To voters, it is them leaving the scene of the crime."
- "Halloween is when kids dress up to scare people. The rest of the year that job belongs to Congress."
- "This Thanksgiving donate your turkey to Congress; at least it will be with its own kind." Also take note; "Washington D.C. in November is known as poultry month, with 535 turkeys and one lame duck."
- "I'm frightened when a candidate says he wants to return the country back to what it used to be. What it used to be was an uninhabited land-mass covered with ice." Fact is, the people who keep referring to the good old days they want to go back to, makes one uneasy, for the frontal lobe portion of their brain must be shrinking. They had better review history.

  Better back when? Oop's! Maybe there was a philosophical fantasy moment with the Grateful Dead, Woodstock, and Timothy Leary?!?! So it should be noted that utopia is never a part of law, finance or economics in this world, or on planet Mongo with Emperor Ming's scientific philosophy. That is why, when it comes to politics; many citizens, particularly business owners, when asked their opinion will give this paraphrased answer: "I wouldn't trust all the King's horses or all the King's men to change a light bulb; let alone put Humpty Dumpty back together again."
- Congress always seems to hit the target, and get the bull's eye when shooting their arrows from their quiver. The why is simple.

They first pick up the bow and shoot the arrow at the target area. Then they approach the target to draw five varying sized circles around the area where the arrow hit the mark. Never, ever a near miss!

- Like the senator said; "Hold that question for now, - so I won't have to answer it later."

Like it or not, big brother is always sipping at everyone's cup of tea. He also has his finger in everyone's dish of porridge, and creates insecurity as to who may be sleeping in one's bed. But he keeps saying, "Not I, not thee; it's that person over there behind the tree." That is why the government has spin doctors just like big business. They are the political operatives that spin the story, and create an alternative reality. The formal term is "Create Fog," by keeping truth and reality under the radar and above the sonar. All this information our government feels is only on a need to know type thing; by keeping people out of their own ignorance operating in a blind spot. Then relaying upon their naïve integrity and lack of due diligence.

Better a "Bah Hum Bug," and reliance first upon one's own self-determination and preservation for business and financial success. That means failing forward by relying upon one's own talents, knowledge, and abilities learned from life's experiences. So for one's learning benefit, there will now be presented first the big macro picture, and then second a smaller micro picture. This is to show and illustrate basic economics, which translates simply into the "transferring of values between entities." Yet, admittedly the macro side tends to be a bit boring and seemingly irrelevant for the majority of working individuals and small business owners. This irrelevant factor must change, and it had better change quickly if the working majority wants to achieve success and maintain their standard of living. Let alone guarantee some semblance of a secure future for their children and grand children.

As stated earlier; the past is prologue with yesterday's remembrances, and many will assume they know about and understand today. But we must prepare everyone we care about and ourselves for tomorrow. Since the next coming of days forward is only imagination and a promissory note; for history does tell us that *"all empires come to an end."*

Now the big picture with following clarifications; less "BRICE"

*** **Supply** ***
[Investment Power Pods]
> Sales/Manufacturing
Research/Development
> *Plus* Innovation.

Government:
Interloper ↕
= Oversight — ON lookers
= Regulate ↔ **{LAW}** ╣ * **observers** *
TAX — * **classroom** *
= Stimulate — (*cost* & *price*) — ON lookers
+Federal Reserve
[*Monetary Control]* ↕

*** **Demand** ***
> Consumption <
[*Buyer/Sold*]

Supply Side: These people have a problem if there are too many goods, and too few buyers. This can develop when there is too much inequity of income. Thus remember this, that the majority of Supply Side people are followers of Adam Smith's Wealth of Nations, Laissez faire philosophy. Let's face it, the rich Supply Side people have a lot to preserve and protect, so they tend to save big time, and do not really trickle down too freely or gratuitously for economic growth. They trickle down with technology, automation, production efficiency and cost containment, and then use charities for tax avoidance and public relations benefits (A great forum for cheap advertizing, and for a positive public image creation.).

Then there is this increasingly active modern day trend of the financially successful, of turning fright capital into flight capital, and voting with their feet. Fact is, our Government encourages and forces travel opportunities. This means citizens first establishing one or more off-shore blind trusts, and then the blind trust sets-up one or more intermediary wealth holding and management trusts. Now the intermediary trust sets-up foreign sales, manufacturing, transfer, reinsurance and banking corporations.

One would be somewhat shocked to know how many rich, wealthy and successful American families have become expats. There is no negative here, for they only lose the right to vote, and never have to sit on a jury. The majority don't worry about the vote issue, for as they often say; "My wallet has more influence with politicians than all my employees votes put together." This is sad but true; since a large number of the members in Congress, and ex-members, have secret and blind off shore accounts to receive undisclosed lobbying dollars, and other influence peddling dollars. Just another annoying fact of life that the average naïve hard working American knows nothing about.

Government and Federal Reserve: What can one say? Both the Government and the Feds tend to talk out of both sides of their mouth, and some people go to the extreme to say they are conjoined twins with the Supply Side controllers. Maybe so, for once a long time ago former President Eisenhower once pre-warned everyone to: "Beware of the Military Industrial Complex." This Eisenhower comment can make one twinge like Gloucester's statement; "As flies to wanton boys, are we to the Gods; they kill us for their sport." But as someone once said; "All evil twins tend to have a good side." The fact is that the Government side has been well presented by John Maynard Keyes with his Keynesians Economic Theory that backs Government intervention when needed. This is mainly to keep the Laissez faire supply siders in line, and provide a somewhat balanced and orderly fairness with protection for the demand consumer.

Of course, this is in complete conflict with the wishful daydreamers at the Chicago School of Economics, Ayn Rand, and at the elite Adam Smith social clubs. The ones who fantasize about trickle down, and leave the markets alone to correct themselves. Of course, they then put the total issue of self-responsibility upon the caveat emptor consumer. Yet, one has to apply some deep thought to appreciate the Federal Reserve thinking on monetary policy, money supply issues, and interest costs related to general borrowing and business loans. These issues have been well covered by economists like John Kenneth Galbraith, Peter Drucker, and Milton Friedman.

Side Line Observers: One can appreciate a good middle of the road moderate. A person with some balanced understanding as to economics being just an over complicated analytical presentation of "Transferring Values." The values being transferred are products and/or services between suppliers (the sellers) and consumers (the buyers). The best here might be British economist John Hobson. Hobson points out that inequity of income causes economic declines when there are too many goods vs. too few buyers. Fact is that the rich can't buy it all, so they save, and they tend to save first to create wealth before buying goods and services. This sheltered savings occasionally disrupts the economic equilibrium, for they do not invest in production or trickle down.

Hobson clearly pointed out that business cycles are based upon fluctuations and ripple effects. With a multiplier effect being that with no business investment, there are no wages; then no buyers for consumption, and then less Supply Side production. Like they say; "What goes around, comes around." So it will not hurt to take a fantasy blink and a glance at Princeton's Economic Game theory, or Columbia's D. Hubbard talent (this guy is quite with it). Then take a moment to look at that funny farm on the Charles River with its slush bucket of brains; like that farmer who was "*out standing* in his field." Fact is, Ralph Waldo Emerson's "Conduct of Life" would make for a good read at this point dealing with economic realities. But please, only with a grain of salt, enjoy the creepy ranting of Ayn Rand; along with her lofty egoist Greek Gods of influence, which inspire her ignorant acolytes to extreme capitalistic views from Mount Olympus. Where lower earthly humans are useless toys.

Demand/Consumers: They tend to be the ones that grease the squeaky wheels, and make the wheels go around. Yet, they also tend to be the ones at the short end of the stick. This is commonly referred to as the Gotcha or Kaput Economics. This situation often occurs with a lack of knowledge without a proper education. It also occurs by enjoying a so-called comfortable status quo existence without having to look back over one's shoulder. Let's face it! There will always be that 10% +/- group referred to as dependency free loaders. Here is where reading a couple works by F. Scott Fitzgerald may be enlightening; the ones concerning his disillusionment views of the American dream for success through hard work and perseverance.

The end result is getting slammed by globalization, a changing world's economic infrastructure, and avoiding to comprehend that "all empires come to an end." Meanwhile many get slammed by either a death, disability, divorce, or dependency (No emergency or retirement dollars.). Then if they are fortunate enough to bypass these trap doors, they get nailed by failing to comprehend the effects of inflation. So let us first look at inflation with a set net income figure of $50,000.00, while using a flat and consistent 4% annual rate of inflation. So to maintain one's standard of living with an equivalent purchasing power of fifty-thousand dollars in the future, one will need; . . .

- **Ten years later;** → will need a net $73,000.00, - or accept a lower devalued purchasing power and standard of living of $37,000.00, if the income stays level @ fifty-thousand dollars.
- **Twenty years down the road;** → will need a net $105,000.00, - or accept a lower purchasing power and standard of living equivalent to $23,700.00, should one's income still be a net fifty-thousand dollars.
- **Thirty years;** → will need $156,000.00, - or be the same in reverse as living on devalued dollars equal to only $15,900.00; this would really be at poverty level if one was looking forward at retirement needs while on a fixed income.

Sad to say, this is one area where ignoring the inflation factor has ruined many a business, and put some totally out of business. Why? They bid out their jobs at the current days prices, and did not factor in future labor, materials, energy, equipment, and/or manufacturing cost. Yes, they were excited when they got the job as the lowest bidder, but they lived to regret it.

So it proves the point that if one cannot forecast money making profits, then let the other person be the non-profit sucker. Don't fall for the purchasing agents' phony promises and projected dreams when they say; "Do this one job (where you underbid and underpriced yourself), and I'll make it up to you later; plus get you a lot of referral business." This is all con-man bull-shit, and one must always remember that purchasing agents eat their young.

One should always remember what Gus Grissom said to reporters before going up into space; "The only thing that worries me is that the government let this job out to the lowest bidder."

Now with inflation out of the way, and Macro out of the way; let us get down to the micro economics. This is the jungle area out there, where "Sand Happens" within one's own personal financial space, and where Big Brother Gov. with Wall Street too often Privatize profits, and Socialize losses.

So when investing for one's current and future needs, one must first analyze what it is they want from the investment; such as <u>CASH FLOW</u>

[interest or dividends], or <u>APPRECIATION</u> [growth as capital gains or ordinary income], or <u>WRITE OFF'S</u> [such as depreciation, depletion allowances, or tax credits], or <u>SAFETY</u> [risk tolerance]. So let us take a look at four risk factors; . . .

1. A person's own ***psychological temperament***, and Psychic Income need, which is translated as Peace of Mind. That is why, if one is not a wealthy high income risk taker; avoid, run for the hills, and away from Private Placements, Trust Deeds, and Ventured Capital deals. The majority are either bogus or losers, and only for Las Vegas type whales.
2. The ***economic risk*** of the stock and bond market. All subject to the Federal Reserve, World Bank, Foreign financial markets, war and peace, the weather, energy prices, and one's own job security. Also that old out-dated, obsolete, and way too low S.E.C & NASD accredited investor rule is just plain crap. Then on the other end of the unbalanced scale is that new, can't catch the fox in the hen house, Portal Group Rule to allow pillage and plunder to continue, and stay deregulated hidden from public view and regulators.
3. ***Tax risk;*** → "<u>CONGRESS</u>," the ones who can shaft investors on very short notice. A perfect historical example would be the 1986 Tax Reform Act. Grandfathered nothing, but at least they did not go retroactive back before January, 1986. Starting late in 1987 thousands of businesses, and thousands of individuals were ruined. They declared various types of bankruptcies, and learned never to trust the Government again when venturing into long term investment commitments.
4. ***Liquidity risk;*** this means the "*staying power*" to ride out the financial turmoil for one or two years. Yes, one can declare tax losses, but a loss, is a loss, is a loss; but it does not put additional food on the table or pay for children's education. So if you cannot ride out a recovery with additional financial resources, - you are screwed, period!

So let us take a short trip down memory lane with Lehman Brothers, the solid Bear Stearns, Freddie Mac and Fannie Mae, A.I.G., WorldCom, Enron, Drexel's B & F'ens' junk bonds, Washington Mutual, Integrated Recourses, Petro Lewis, and over one-hundred and forty-seven life insurance companies. We can also add into this mix over one-hundred well known investment and brokerage firms. There is no such thing as 100% safe, secured, and guaranteed. So never forget this question; "Guaranteed by Who?"

The next investment decision is; what does one want to happen with their wealth creation dollars? Now here again we are presented with another four considerations.

1. **DEFER** (tax delay, use later down the road): This area is placing dollars in Pensions, I.R.A.'s, Annuities, or long term investments holds in real estate. This could also be in numismatics or philately(ist).
2. **CONVERT** (change the tax status of earning): Here one desires to change investment earnings from Ordinary Income taxable to Capital Gains Income, or to Tax Free income. This can also include non-recapturing government tax-free credit income against income taxes.
3. **DEDUCT** (write-off's): Taken as depreciation, expenses, tax credits, or depletion allowances [referred to as expensing a wasting asset as with oil and gas wells, or by filling up a valuable empty hole in the ground with waste or garbage.].
4. **DIVERT**: Simply means transfer an asset with valuable growth and/or income potential to another person, business entity, or some designed charitable structure to be taxed at a much lower tax bracket. A good example would be a small business S-Corp. that is making a nice small excess profit of $50,000.00, so with wise counsel this small business owner elects to become a fiscal year 1120 C-"Corp. WOW!! Now that the excess profits are taxed at 15% +/-, rather than one's personal tax bracket of say 35% +/-; the wise business owner now uses this move to create more beautiful net cash flow.

Therefore, the more success one achieves, the more one must recognize and understand to some degree Macro →> **"BRICE."** For a slight misunderstanding of the BRICE affect can even kill off small business owners.

Fact is that all economics, finances, and laws are interconnected, whether one likes it or not, with Brazil, Russia, India, China, and Europe. China in this group is 'Puff the Magic Dragon,' and sometimes the dragon wins. The winning part in this multi-national corporate world globalization economy is with rare earth elements, energy resources, and commodity labor. Here is where China holds a near monopoly in this critical arena, particularly with high tech products. This is why multi-international businesses are diversifying and relocating into China, and with the rest of the BRI-E, -RI-E, -R–E.

Thus, international and national laws are at the center of the mix, and quite often legal minds become the power behind the throne. Since labor has become the new hot commodity, the age of the "B" student with a nice comfortable career is fading, and the "C" student; forget it!! But take comfort in the fact that it is still not too late to learn, and get smarter with learned experiences. For the future high priced value is for those individuals with good people skills, quality knowledge between the ears, and who are bilingual.

Wealthy people and solid businesses will pay small fortunes to learn what they don't know to protect and preserve their success. Therefore, the one who has that secret and elusive knowledge hidden and locked between their ears receives the big check, and happily grins all the way to the bank. But particularly the person who really understands this George Bernard Shaw comment; "I have always questioned the courage of a lion tamer, for he is always in a cage where people cannot get at him."

So a key for success is to get out of the cage, off one's dead apathy, and quit saying tomorrow. It does not take much thought to realize that this is tomorrow and the first day of the rest of your life. This brings back a statement a child made to his parents after falling out of bed; "I guess I fell asleep too near where I got in." For at this moment, you're younger than you will ever be again, and you're older than you have ever been.

That is why one must get wiser with common sense, wake up to reality, and not allow themselves to fall asleep mentally tomorrow. So in a weird sense, that is why one cannot ignore government issues or politicians. For as successful individuals, we are not merely to endure change, nor even to profit by it, but to cause it. So curiously enough, since the best cream always rises to the top of the milk; some people can always do the best things, in the worst of times. One may hate to say it, but this often applies to politicians we may not like. You know, the ones that occasionally give us comfort and peace of mind as business owners.

There was this Congressman, a friendly neighbor, who was always bragging about liking youth, and always campaigning for school issues and community youth programs. One day he laid a fresh concrete driveway, and before it dried, kids put initials and handprints in it. Boy was this congressman mad. While making foul comments, and condemning the kids, his wife said: "I thought you liked kids?" His answer was; "I do in the abstract, but not in the concrete." Yet, this is the way politicians like their voters and campaign contributors; "In the abstract!" To think otherwise would be kidding one's self, and pulling the wool over one's own eyes. But enjoy the ride.

There will be many times one realizes that the only thing they have in common with a politician is that they both breathe, and want to say; "Sir, have you considered putting back in a wisdom tooth?" This was so true some years back when Congress passed a tax law referred to as E.R.I.S.A., and it soon became the Attorneys Fair Employment Act. Then the new E.R.I.S.A. tax law became known as "Every Ridiculous Idea Since Adam." It proved to be just that, with negative consequences affecting all in our current times.

This ridiculousness is why there are these four key political economic terms one must be cognizant of if planning to become successful as a financier or business owner. The four are; Redistributionist, Reallocationist, Revenue Enhancements, and Social Reactionaries. We just won't get into the various Depopulationist principles as to the world's growing over-population issues. That is why one should never forget the two part break down of the word ***POLITICS***; > *where* "**Poli**" ↔ many, and "**tics**" ↔ blood suckers.

Lest one should forget; while living, the government collects the interest on one's success. Then upon one's death they call in the principal. Fact is though, we don't want to become too pessimistic, but the Bible did say that God created the world in six days, and on the seventh day he rested. Please take note: It did not say he celebrated. God knew he could have completed his work in four days, and rested on the fifth, sixth and seventh day; but he was delayed by trying to decide and figure out what to do about Nevada, West Virginia, Poland and Kentucky.

Oh, what the heck! Facts are facts, reality is reality, and it does no one any good to wear blinders. Naiveté should not block awareness that many of our idols and leaders have feet of clay as follows; - Which group is it?

So far; 41 arrested for spousal abuse. 16 arrested for fraud. 27 wrote bad checks. 117 directly or indirectly were involved in the bankrupting of at least two companies. 6 spent time in jail for assault. 91 can not get a credit card because of bad credit. 23 arrested on drug charges. 11 arrested for shoplifting. 23 were named defendants in lawsuits just recently in one year alone, and 17 with serious sexual perversion issues. Oh what the heck, even the Holy Knight's of Ore had their *page* issues? Yet, this does not even include current investigations involving unethical and possibly corruption issues, or holier than thou secret side street issues; - as if religion provides an Old Testament exemption?

So what group of holier than thou individuals do these people come from? Here is a clue. They were justifiably called the House of the Corrupt for many a year. Even then a general officer was not even wise enough to use the Vesco Law when he was luckily caught at the end of the Abscam food chain. Yet many others in Congress had/have secrets upon secret plantations and bank accounts in places like Saint Martine, Dominican Republic, Costa Rica, Martinique, Andorra, and Liechtenstein. Yet for fairness and balance, some of our so-called honorable lifetime appointed Federal Judges also collect their rewards for good decision making somewhere else unknown.

But to be fair, one should not pick upon only the national politicians and federal jerky public employees who unethically abuse the system. There are plenty of County Commissioners, State Legislators, and City Council Members that have their hands in the teal, or stretched out for kick-in's or kick backs. The only real sad part is, when they find those few trusted policemen and firemen cheating, and unethically abusing the system; with pay-off's, overtime and sick leave abuse, phony expenses, and occasionally embezzling from their own pension or union trust funds. All done at the tax payer's expense, and too often proving that there is no honor among *none* thieves.

Maybe this closing story tells, and makes a subtle point: There was this poor street person living in a small southern Alabama town. He was known as the town dummy, while standing in the same area everyday for years. The towns' people enjoyed him as entertainment, and as the idiot jester. This northern businessman while visiting the town to work with clients, was quickly introduced to the dummy for show and entertainment by several of the local wealthy business clients. They wanted to introduce the stranger to the dummy for some humor, and to show how ignorant he was.

They said; "Watch this." Then, one client placed a dime and a nickel in the palm of his hand, and told the dummy that he could only take one of the coins to keep. The dummy took the nickel, and the locals started laughing out loud over this incident while walking back to their offices. One explained; "See how dumb this guy is, for he always takes the nickel because it is bigger, and he is too dumb to know the dime has more value."

Later after business meetings, the northern businessman was walking back to his motel, and ran into the town dummy. He asked the old man if he could speak to him for a minute. He said to the town dummy, after taking a nickel and dime out of his pocket and holding it openly in the palm of his hand; "Sir, I'd first like to apologize for the people that introduced me to you. I'd like to help you understand and know that the dime, not this larger nickel, has more value." The nice old gentleman interrupted and stopped the northern businessman from talking, and said; "Sur! I'es knows the difference, but if I'es takes the dime, they will stop playing the game."

CHAPTER V

Awareness of legalities and rules that you must learn to use, and live with.

The sub-title to this section could be "Et Tu Brute," for it points out the fact that people are too often hurt by to much trust. This violation of trust is quite often served up and provided on an expensive platter by so-called trusted individuals within the legal and accounting professions. Therefore, one must remember the basic fact that always places the primary burden of proof upon you. That burden is, "Ignorance of the law is no excuse." So it is actually your fault should you retain an incompetent, unethical, ignorant lawyer, accountant, or financial advisor.

The following information learned cannot keep the dogs from barking, but it can keep the dogs from biting you. So in a strange twisted way the "Rocky Horror Picture Show" cut to the chase, and to the quick with "I can remove the cause, but not the symptoms."/ "You're spaced out on sensation, like you're under sedation." Yeah! The old saying is right even if one often gets frustrated and bored; - "It is as you wish it, or it is what it is." So let's hope it is not the other saying of "Too soon old, too late smart."

There are many cases where the defendants took a punishing loss in the courts, even though they thought they had good legal advice, but the judge ruled that "Ignorance of the law is no excuse." One particular case stands out to make the point. The case, Welhelm v. Comm.; where after the judge ruled against the defendant, he said: "What were you paying these lawyers for? This presents a very sad fact, which seems too often to be relevant. That is the more incompetent the lawyer, the more money the lawyer seems to make.

Now sadly, this is like so many other legal horror stories. It's a high priced example of incompetency with supervised neglect. Here, as with most similar situations, the naive client rehired the same lawyer who had originally given them the improper advice. WOW! The incompetent lawyer now gets to double bill their client again, just to defend their own erroneous advice. Lawyers like this would take the pennies off their dead mother's eyes, and then accuse the funeral director of doing it. Oh well, maybe this observation is a little too harsh when we need to remember that law is an adversarial system, and that fifty-percent (or half) of all lawyers lose their cases.

You will now be treated to some short condensed to the point stories, that are truthful and factual horror stories dealing with the legal and accounting profession. After these short and brief tales of reality, you will start to learn, appreciate, and understand the legal points at issue with these stories. Hopefully one will then become aware of bear trap issues, and learn how to avoid similar situations in their life.

Therefore, the legal points provided within this chapter will be beneficial and help one protect their future success. Of course, the legal points provided may also be used wisely to benefit one's family, friends and associates. But with caution, remember the statement in the book "Of Mice and Men;' - "The best laid plans of mice and men often go astray." With this said, one will soon learn a very key subjective word that is applicable with any type of planning, and that word is HOWEVER. And yes, there is always the rare exception, but do not bank on, or count on the exception to save the rear end.

So let's get started with the thought provoking stories to illustrate that the Holy Roman Empire of rape, pillage and plunder may still exist with certain professions. Maybe that is why Dieogeoniese might still be out there late at night with his lamp, wandering around in the dark looking for an honest person. For within the legal arena there is always this conflict between legal vs. right, since something can be 100% legal, and 100% unethical at the same time.

These following incidents of harm done to innocent and unsuspecting people will provide you, the reader, an indirect and harmless way to have a productive learning experience. But while reading the following, think about this question now asked; "What happens if you should make a mistake by living?"

Story #1 - Lawyer works the nursing homes and assisted living facilities, and does free presentations, and $29.00 wills. He got caught with his hand in the cookie jar. He named himself beneficiary on our elderly woman's document. Oop's! She died, and he got $250,000.00 tax free. Now what did the Bar Association do? A joke! They fined him $2,500.00, and gave him a letter of reprimand not to do it again. Wow! - Nice profit for being unethical and crooked.

The sad fact about this type of incident is that the author has seen this same rip off of elderly people by lawyers at least a dozen times. One lawyer was even an elected state legislator. All these lawyers accomplished unjust enrichment, and got away with it, with only a mild slap on their wrist. So apparently it is very profitable for lawyers to be acting as undertakers for the living, walking elderly that are not dead yet.

Story #2 - Lawyer works in a law firm assisted in closing down a huge estate where the rich man died, and left behind a lonely, sad, naïve wealthy widow. The widow had additional grief because her two children had previously died. This lawyer took pity upon her, visited her regularly, took her to church, out to dinner regularly, and became her phony soul mate. Within two years, this young lawyer convinced the wealthy elderly women to adopt him. She did, the lawyer quit practicing law, and has now become a new potentially wealthy heir. Clearly, a wolf in sheep's clothing. Hope he is not a black widower type heir.

Story #3 - C.P.A accountant convinces all his brilliant talented clients, who were sadly ignorant, naïve and trusting, to let his firm handle all their business affairs. The C.P.A. firm handled all the office management, the payroll, then established and managed the pension plans. They arranged for all the insurance coverage's needed, did all their taxes, and in some cases even paid their personal bills. Wow! The C.P.A. did it all, and the professional business owners could not be happier doing only their wonderful specialty work. Why not? This C.P.A. was indirectly endorsed by a major university, by agents with a major insurance company, and two questionable law firms. Oh by the way, he paid off and manipulated the two law firms, and the insurance agents. Suddenly the I.R.S. is looking at the accounting practices of this questionable character. A crook with a so-called respectable reputation within the charity community.

Oop's! - This wonderful accountant vanished to Spain, with over $50,000,000.00 of the clients' money that just vanished into thin air, and Spain has a no extradition policy. So while he is living fat and sassy on the Spanish Riviera, several of his former clients committed suicide, and a couple declared bankruptcy. Yet, all should have spent more time reading and analyzing the story of the "Three Little Pigs."

Story #4 - A lawyer with the accountant's help manipulated a successful business owner who was too trusting and naïve. They upon his death took over and owned his business free and clear. This is a prime case and a perfect example where one must learn that a friendly social relationship in a lodge, community social club, or a country club does not have the "Good Housekeeping Seal of Approval." The unethical game started at the beginning, when the advisors made the new business owner think that he needed to give them a little stock (2 ½ % each), and also put them on his board to qualify as a formal C-Corp.

Once this poor sucker's success hit big time, the trusted lawyer and accountant advised him to buy a key man corporate owned life insurance policy for $1,500,000.00, and along with it execute a stock redemption agreement. The agreement would have the corporation buy back family inherited stock with the tax free insurance dollars, so that there would be sufficient funds to pay any and all estate settlement costs. This practice is commonly referred to as a 303 stock redemption. But with underhanded sneakiness, these advisors drew up, and had executed a 302 stock redemption that the naïve business owner signed.

It also helped the advisors to know that the wife of the business owner cared little about the business. She was a twit housewife with the I.Q. of a tulip, and preferred tennis and cards at the country club with other naïve and ignorant wives. But sadly, the unexpected now happened. The nice successful business owner had an aneurysm, and died. So the poet Browning may have got it right with; "Just when we feel the safest, there comes a sunset's touch."

This touch of the dragon now left the lawyer and accountant as the new 100% owners of a successful corporation worth over three million, and it did not cost them a dime. They just used the corporate life insurance the owner basically paid for with his corporate dollars, and paid it out tax-free to the appreciative, ignorant widow and her children that just got screwed. Since the corporation on her behalf collected the $1.5-million. Then she the widow surrendered the so-called inherited stock back to the corporation in order to receive the $1.5-million per the skullduggery subterfuge 302 redemption agreement. So now the widow has just been disinherited and conned out of her inherited family stock.

This whole scenario just proves that dead people receive little or no respect and loyalty, and that consciously influencing innocent people in order to commit conscious fraud is very prevalent. The sad fact is that too many advisors prefer to keep their clients operating in a blind spot.

This author has run across this scam three other times, and stopped it before anyone died. Needless to say, the lawyers involved had no love for me, once they were exposed for their unethical plans to remove the gold coins off the dead man's eyes. The disappointment factor was that with two of the other 302 redemption frauds, the lawyers were partners in big reputable law firms, and the accountants involved were partners in some so-called Big Eight or Six accounting firms. The existence of unethical, incompetent, and over charging partners within these big accounting firms is just way too common of a practice.

Story #5 - This one will blow one's mind. A widower worth $2,200,000.00 goes to a local steak house for a free meal, and a free Estate Planning seminar. They stated that since he recently moved into the state, that he needed a new updated will and trust. Their lawyers' usual fee was $695.00, but if he signed up for their services that evening, the fee would only be $495.00. They told him that since he had no relatives in the state, they would act as personal representative and trustee since the law firm had a trust company. Then to make him feel secure, they told him they could make his brother first advisor to the trust, and then his children. But bad things just seem to happen for the benefit of discounting, hustling lawyers when the senior citizens unexpectedly die.

Now whether one likes it or not, this case proves that money has become the focus of law, - not justice. This lawyer and his firm legally got away with charging and receiving $600,000.00 to settle the estate. So piracy just keeps hanging around with the dead on the yard arms, and the heirs walking the plank.

Story #6 - This very nice senior citizen widow, with a nice sized estate unfortunately had a nice, helpful and friendly neighbor for over 15 years. The neighbor just happened to be an attorney. Now the widow had two problems. One, she had very poor eyesight; and two, a nice neighbor who volunteered to update her estate planning. They did it alright, with the nice neighbor named as executor. The will with a trust contained numerous special bequests to relatives and charities. But shockingly at the end of the trust document, there was this sentence; "All residual assets remaining in the estate and not distributed by the grantor's specific bequest, shall be distributed without encumbrances or claims to the; ... Guess who? Another named partner lawyer in the law firm.

Story #7 - This one takes the cake. A business owner was emotionally suffering along with his wife who was dying of cancer over the previous two years prior to her death. He spent a quarter million dollars on quacks in U.S., Mexico, Jamaica, and in Italy. All being misled by unethical U.S. doctors that co-owned foreign miracle clinics. The law firm that worked on settling the wife's estate used a young lawyer, who spotted the heartbroken and lonely "Golden Goose." Within two years she manipulated his emotions, and became his new pregnant spouse with a nowhere to be found pre/post marital agreement. She now became a successful "Jacqueline in the Bean Stock," immediately quit the practice of law to become a community socialite. Oh yes! After she quickly divorced her common place lover and hard working printer press husband.

Story #8 - This wonderful, charitably oriented plastic surgeon did not stay home to run the very successful family business. His widowed mother continued to operate the business with the help of good management personnel. His elderly mother died, he was with her at the end, and after the funeral had gone to see their old family lawyer. The lawyer stated he had not been the lawyer for the firm or his mother for well over two years.

Now what strange happenings became afoot to entangle mother's estate? For unbeknownst to the doctor, and even to his sister; a local Holy Roller fundamentalist tent preacher got involved with the mother's life. This outside influence began with the hiring of a regular house keeper that belonged to this church. This housekeeper somehow got the mother thinking about the sweet bye and bye, rather than the nasty now and now. Then the pastor and fellowship members began to visit the mother regularly, and invited her into their church.

You may have guessed it already. The doctor and his sister received none of the wealthy estate. You see, nine months earlier the pastor with the church lawyer rewrote the mother's will, and left 100% of everything to the pastor's church.

So believe this or not; this religious abuse and trickery by Pastors, Rabbis' and Priest is a very common practice throughout all religious groups. Also, there have been several well-known 'big time evangelists' that have capitalized upon this practice of religious abuse many times.

Story #9 - The dean of a well known medical and dental school put together a team of crooked lawyers, accountants, investment people, and then started holding seminars all over the U.S. Most attendees were general dentists, oral surgeons, orthodontists and periodontists. All the doctors were great practitioners in their profession, but dumber than a box of rocks about everything else.

This trusted dean of the medical and dental school ripped off his clients for millions, and got most of them in deep trouble with the I.R.S. Yes, he went to prison. He is now out on the street again, and practicing his profession upon naïve, innocent and trusting patients in another state; SAD!

Story #10 - There was this wonderfully kind, religious and wealthy client who had been on a kidney dialysis program for several years. But he was now at his end days in a special kidney care unit at the hospital, and under the regular care of two highly trained resident doctors in this specialty field.

They catered to him, and made him feel like they were his two lost sons. They overly convinced him that they would dedicate their lives at finding a cure, and still treat people properly who lacked financial resources for proper medical care. They must have cried that they were currently too poor, and lacked the proper resources to advance and promoted their care to needy patients.

The dying man soon died while at the hospital. Later while his attorney was working on the estate, he noticed that the man had written two separate checks, one to each doctor for $275,000.00. Needless to say, he went looking for the doctors, but they resigned their positions at the hospital right after the checks cleared, and they went west. At this point in my career, I thought I had seen it all, and that nothing would surprise me. I was wrong, for this one took the cake. The two doctors did not even hang around to see the man die, or help at the end time to provide consoling comfort once those checks had cleared.

Story #11 - How would you like to have purchased an 800 acre farm worth about five-hundred thousand dollars at the time, for little or nothing? There was this well known lawyer who pulled it off. This lonely senior citizen widow had to now manage the farm once her farmer husband died. She could not farm it, so she leased out the land by the acre, and regularly had to hire people to maintain the up-keep and maintenance on the buildings and equipment.

Please guess who became her very best friend? Yep! It was the lawyer and his staff who settled her husband's estate. He visited her regularly, and had his staff stop around regularly to make sure she was okay. The staff also made sure there was proper handling of the land lease contracts, and on time payment receipts from the leasees. Then one day the lawyer convinced her that he wanted to be a farmer, and that he would like to buy the farm from her since none of her children lived on the farm, wanted the farm, or lived within the state. He assured her that she would have a very secure retirement income based upon the installment sales agreement to purchase the farm. He also made her feel extra secure and comfortable, by letting her know she could remain living on the farm free and clear with no rent payments or other costs until she dies.

This idea was music to the widow's ears, as a gift from heaven, and she quickly made the deal. She quickly and joyfully signed the very thick twenty-five or thirty page contract without consulting other counsel. Oop's! This Foxy-Loxy lawyer had nailed down his one sided installment sales, and made his regular monthly payments on time, or ahead of time. He was a real happy camper, and then forty-one months later he was jumping for joy because the nice elderly lady died. The payments now legally ended, the installment sale was complete, and he now legally owned the farm free and clear. For this smooth con-job installment sale is referred to legally as a Private Annuity Sale and/or a Self-cancelling Installment Note. So upon her death the sale was considered completed with no further payments over the next 16 years, and no residual money or payments due to the heirs.

Story #12 - Now for the final dirty dozen story. This one is why the author went back to continue his education and obtain a Law Degree. My grandfather was a very successful farmer, and a shrewd successful business man. At the age of 83, he started having some mild dementia.

This was not noticeable to anyone, unless they were quite familiar with him or around him on a regular basis. Sadly, this was noticed by his attorney, accountant, and his much younger business partner. They were supposedly long term trusted friends socializing together at the Odd Fellows Lodge, and at the Masonic Temple. But my grandfather's advisors soon realized that their future was going to be with his younger business partner. So as a group one nice sunny day, they took my grandfather out to lunch to make him feel good. Then after lunch they escorted him directly to the County Court House, where he appeared to people working there as normal.

Their plan was working perfectly; for these so-called trusted advisors and lodge friends had him sign off as fully paid, millions of dollars in personal record notes for money he had loaned to their corporation. This money was not a contribution to capital, and the advisors also doctored the corporate minute books to state that the corporation had months earlier redeemed my grandfather's stock. If my grandfather would not have died too soon for them, they might have gotten away with it.

Now my mother, who was the only heir, was naïve and lived out of state, but she just felt something was rotten in Denmark. So she retained an influential retired judge to handle her interest, and research all aspects of her father's business. Bingo! The judge found out and exposed all of the underhanded dealings, bankrupted all the parties involved, and filed criminal charges. But between inheritance taxes, federal estate taxes, legal fees and uncollectible monies due from the crooks; there was very little left in the estate for my mother.

So the only real gratification that came out of this ridiculous set of unethical actions, was that the attorney, the accountant and business partner were found guilty, and they all went to prison for a very long time. All thanks to a retired probate Judge Bell.

•

Most of these questionable legal ethical issues became more understandable and apparent when observed at a Miami Estate Tax Institute attended by about eight-hundred lawyers. The speaker was a top respected lawyer and professor on legal ethics around estate and probate issues. This speaker started his one hour presentation, but after twenty-five minutes the room was near empty. At least ninety-percent of the attendees walked out on the speaker in a varying unprofessional manner, and while leaving the room made subtle, impolite departing comments. At the end, most of the lawyers left the room, but about sixty *attorneys* remained to applaud the speaker's fine presentation.

Now if there was a thirteenth story, it would have to be a separate novel about incompetent, unethical, and so-called professional life insurance agents. Those people who were given a low I.Q. state license for passing a simple kindergarten exam. And yes it is true, that they had additional marketing, sales, and policy training for several weeks on how to get their foot inside one's front door. Then how to close the sale, fill out the policy application, and collect the premiums. So when they got the big commission it was well earned, - maybe? Since cold calling and prospecting is hard work and often very frustrating at the beginning of one's insurance career, after first selling all their relatives and close friends crap.

Therefore, should one be sympathetic to their plight? Do not think so if they are claiming to be professional life underwriters dealing with farmers, business owners, professionals and other successful people. The fact is, if someone is not so successful, near poor, has few assets with a small or medium estate; then selling the policy rightly or wrongly will have little, if any, negative effect. The warning now is, that down the road in the future should one become successful, that policy may become the kiss of death and a creative liability.

But first, stories about several crooked insurance agents honored and protected with cover-up payments by their companies. Why? The damages paid out were far less than the massive premiums the producing agents brought into the companies every year. But first a warning; never pay the premiums directly to the agent or his agency. Only write premium checks directly to the insurance company.

- Agent one had his new clients write a first quarterly premium check to his agency to activate the policy immediately upon underwriters approval. Oop's! - The agent wrote a $3-million dollar policy, got the first big quarterly premium paid in advance to his agency, but sent the policy into the company as C.O.D. The agent now got paid his full commission, plus the unearned and illegal keeping of the first quarterly premium. Guess what? The big corporate executive client died within the ninety days, and the client company thought upon the policy delivery that they would be paying the second quarterly premium. Wrong! They filed a troubling death claim that was rejected. The insurance company quickly sent the agent and his wife on an extended vacation out of the state for over three months until the issue got a confidential settlement.

- Two separate agents with two weird incidents. One wrote insurance on bridges for the state, and another wrote commercial property insurance. Both always billed the insurance premiums from their agency, and had premiums paid to their agency. Oop's! For one agent a major bridge collapsed, and there was no insurance. For the other agent a tornado hit the small downtown, and the business owners had no coverage.

  These agents printed up and issued phony contracts in the name of the insurance companies they represented. The agents were rich by living off the total premiums paid for over ten years by their clients with no real coverage. Let's face it, who would have thought a major bridge would collapse, and that a small tornado would hit a nice little rural town's business district.

- An agent wrote a $250,000.00 life insurance policy, and the insured man was accidently killed. The good looking widow did not know that the policy had a double indemnity clause, and that it would pay out $500,000.00. The over sexed married agent told the grieving widow that he could arrange for her and the kids to get a lot more money out of the insurance company than the $250,000.00. The catch was that she would have to remain very silent and quiet, and also kick back to him $100,000.00. Their scheme got exposed; the widow got all the money due, and the life insurance company's number one top agent for over five years kept on writing business for the company. All was forgiven.

So let us start off easy while going down the "Yellow Brick Road" towards learning the needed legalities of life to cover one's ass. The why is so you won't be spending time looking over your shoulder while nearing the castle, or while you're living peacefully within your castle of success. But first let's take note for damage recovery against incompetent or unethical life insurance agent mistakes. The LAW clearly states that the statute of limitation for life insurance blunders does not start running until the damage occurs or when the damage is realized. This usually happens upon one's death, so the agent and company who sold the policy back 5, 10, 15 years ago now becomes totally liable for his, hers, or their past incompetency.

Let us first talk about Code Section 2042. This section of law is referred to as **"Incidents of Ownership."** Should one screw up here, then all the vultures get rich due to their ignorance of the law. This section 2042 states that if you personally are the owner and have control over your life insurance policy it may well be subject to Federal Estate Taxes of (give or take) around 35% to 55%. This all depends upon how the winds of Congress blow, and how their created deficit grows. Yet, a point of clarity: Life insurance is only state estate tax free, but it is not necessarily federal estate tax free. This taxing fact has destroyed many a family farm or family business. **Wow!** What a shocking realization that the Government always levies upon poor advice **(Code Section 6332(b).**

Now maybe a factual incident will teach one about other needed code sections at law. The following lesson is provided to you by a C.L.U. idiot career life insurance agent. So as the story goes, the agent had written an $850,000.00 high premium policy, on which this agent received a 55% commission plus a 35% expense bonus commission. A CEBA professional was retained to do a complete review of this very successful person's financial and legal affairs. This client had several troubling issues, and one was the Incidents of Ownership problem with his life insurance policy.

Then at the presentation, unknown to the CEBA, he invited over his fraternity brother life insurance agent that sold this policy to him. Right away this C.L.U. clown attacked him, and stated; "This policy is not subject to taxation as you stated, and you as well as I know that all life insurance is tax free in this state. Also, since they are married, the policy proceeds, should my client die first, would be 100% tax free under the "Unlimited Marital Deduction Credit" allowed between spouses.

The CEBA's response was first to set the trap, and use the agent's mistake to kill him off by making him foolishly play in the CEBA's ballgame. First, he congratulated the agent for selling the policy to fulfill his fraternity brother's estate needs. Then he cut him off at the knees. One, the CEBA informed him that his client only had simple wills, and the wills included a 30 day common disaster clause. This meant that if killed in a common disaster, the I.R.S. would take half the children's needed money, since this clause in the will makes the assumption the other spouse died first. - Oop's!

Point two: The CEBA said; I guess you were not told or informed, or failed to ask the question about their marital status. Or maybe you just did not know the effect their pre-marital agreement would have upon the taxation of the policy proceeds. - Oop's! The agent was then reminded that the pre-marital agreement as to Federal Estate Taxes left the firm assumption that the couple had no Unlimited Marital Deduction for protection of the insurance proceeds.- Oop's!

Now it just got ridiculously worse for this agent. He mistakenly opened his mouth and cut his own throat. He immediately said; "No problem here, I will just have you sign an amendment form to correct the oversight, and it will make your wife the "Owner if other than the insured." Now we have here another lesson to be learned. That lesson is Code Section 2035b; this section clearly states that if one corrects a found error such as this one with their life insurance policy; the correction will not be effective or take effect for three (3) years. - Oop's!

Goodbye ex-fraternity friend. Now the CEBA made sure the policy was properly rewritten at a far lower premium. Then made sure the client had new wills and trusts properly executed, along with proper real estate titling to avoid probate. This successful person, his wife, and his children are now much safer.

Now for those key Code Sections at law that are simple to know, find, and understand. The why is for the safety of one's family, one's assets, and one's personal success. These particular Code Sections at law are staples within the system, and have not been changed for many a year. Plus, they are not likely to be modified in the near future with any major tax legislation. The why is that they have no noticeable political voting significance. Also, they are the hidden and unnoticed bear traps within the system that only tend to effect the successful person, or wealthy family. So the following rules are not going to go away. Therefore, you and your family do not want to pay a nasty price in the future for being unaware of, and for ignoring these rules and regulations, regardless of what Congress may or may not do down the road.

These following Code Sections are the unseen annoying mosquito, hornet, or killer bee that can really irritate when they bite and sting.

Section 2042 - Incidents of Ownership: By the way, this rule also applies to corporate life insurance (individual, but not group) should one be a 50% or more owner of the corporation. Then if it is key man corporate life insurance, one must have up-to-date corporate minutes to state the insurance is an operation asset so it will not inflate the corporate stock value. If not mentioned, the insurance will be considered a non-operating asset, and this can be a real valuation problem.

Section 2035(b) - the three (3) year limitation and restriction rule when correcting life insurance errors.

Section 6332(b) - What so-called asset protection? The I.R.S. [the government] can levy directly on a life insurance or annuity policy's cash values "without" a foreclosure suit. All they need to do is serve notice upon the insurance company, and the insurance company must pay over all your cash value money to the government within 90 days.

There is one very easy competency test to find out if your life insurance agent is worth his salt. Just open up the policy, go to the back and look at the copy of your original application for insurance. Now go to the bottom of the page where you signed the application. Do you see only one signature down there (yours), or is there underneath your signature a second signature (owner if other than insured)? Now if one is successfully well off, one had better hope there is a third signature as a contingent owner.

This third signature is security protection should the second owner (usually a spouse) die first. Maybe more important is if the second owner became disabled (usually a spouse), and power of attorney is exercised over the second owner by the insured owner. Oop's! - Incidents of Ownership would revert back to the insured unless there is that contingent owner.

Why? Quite simple, the insured person now has power and control back over the second signature person who was the designated owner. Enough about legal life insurance issues, so we move on to will and trust issues.

We will start with basic code sections, and then play some mind games with you, to make sure you're smarter than the average lawyer bear.

Code Sections 2002, 3467, 6018, 25.2502-2, 25.6019-1(c), plus numerous tax cases and Revenue Ruling to back up the following points. These sections refer to ***Oop's!*** > **Executor and/or Personal representative total liability issues when dealing with a deceased person's probate.** Here is an area where one does not want to screw-up. Why? Because you want to avoid 'Post Mortem' estate planning after the fact, and not have someone playing around with your money at your spouse's and children's' expense.

Oh, by the way! Should you become a successful person with substantial assets like a family farm or business, one of the out-of-context statements made by ignorant estate marketing people and insurance agents is that trusts avoid probate 100%. Not quite! The trust may in some way avoid some assets going through a local probate *(Probate One),* but should you be a financially successful person, your estate would most likely be subject to *Probate Two.*

Now bordering and invading in this strange government land of Probate Two is where lawyers only tend to react, and never create. For most are old school incompetent lawyers, and too often feel threatened by creativity and change. Since it may not be their wanted and controlling old fashioned idea, they are against it. Particularly should it affect their future uncontrollable time clock billings?

That is why it would be nice just once to find a one-handed lawyer. Where they do not always say this, but then this and that on one hand, then go and pronounce; "But, on the other hand?!?!"

The Probate Two is the #706 **Federal Estate Tax Probate procedure** that starts basically after most of the work is completed in about six to nine months with *Probate One.* Now this is where the lawyers and accountants really roll in the big bucks! So one of the ways to slow down and stop the probate abuse, and keep the estate settle cost at a minimum, is to understand the pattern of the following three questions, since failure to understand the intent behind these three questions will destroy your "Chinese Wall" of protection for your family and other heirs.

Attorney: >? "Who would you like to be your executor/personal representative, and/or trustee for your estate?"

You the client: >? "Who should it be?"/ "What do you think?"

Attorney response: >!! "It should be someone you love and trust." Oop's! - A gotcha statement.

One's answer now as the client, will crack a hole in the Chinese wall of protection, and slightly open a Pandora's Box to cause additional emotional grief and unwanted financial headaches for one's spouse and heirs. The fact is, that the answer stating my spouse, or any other individual can be the kiss of death. The often made joke is that this provides automatic malpractice protection for the lawyer. The lawyer or accountant screws up the estate work that your heirs are paying them for, and they make a $57,000.00 mistake. Who is held liable for the $57,000.00 mistake; the lawyer, the accountant, or one's spouse as the executor? Wrong!! It will be your spouse as executor, while becoming a varying modern story of the Lawyer Spider and the Spouse Fly.

Now here is that issue of "Ignorance of the law is no excuse." While another key issue is how much bonding coverage protection does one's lawyer or accountant have? Yes, you can sue the advisors later on, but one will have just created more grief, and only get a slight recovery after several hassling years.

Oh yes! Who should be the executor or personal representative? That is an easy answer. First, should the net estate be under $250,000.00 plus or minus depending upon one's state's laws, this falls into the category of a no administration estate, or sight administration estate. So one can do it themselves if not emotionally distraught, and have some degree of intelligence.

One just takes a copy of the will, a death certificate, and a listing of all the deceased person's assets at their true current stated appraised value to the probate department at the Court House. One then answers a few questions, certifies a couple of forms, pays $100.00 up to maybe $300.00, and the probate estate is closed. **Fact**: The people at the court house; the clerks, judges, and the administrators are not your enemy. They usually are very kind, thoughtful, and helpful beyond expectations. The issue is not to avoid probate, but to avoid probate lawyers. The enemies on the courthouse steps, that will open the doors into misery, are these vulturine seedy lawyers.

Probate is not the boogey man. The ghost in the closet and the scary skeletons under the bed are the wallet goblin probate lawyers. Yes, the many horror stories are true, but don't blame probate or the people working within the probate court system. The complications are usually created mostly by the deceased person's own negligence and ignorance prior to death by doing nothing to protect and preserve assets for the potential heirs.

Now you're a person with a much larger estate. So *only* name a bank trust company as the executor, - period. If you also have a trust, *only* name the bank trust company as sole trustee upon death, since while you are alive, you are your own trustee with no cost or fees. But then for your comfort zone, name your spouse and/or adult children advisor(s) to the trust once activated upon death, and grant them the power to fire the bank trust as the corporate trustee.

You say why? The bank trust has the knowledge and experience, plus unlimited bonding protection. They also are a neutral party, controlled by very strict banking laws, and they do not get sick, disabled mentally or physical, die, or have *addiction problems*. Another real benefit is that they cannot be influenced or swayed by undue influences of friends, religious leaders, neighbors, a conniving lawyer, and in particular the In-laws.

But to be fair, should the estate be medium in size and not so large to have #706 *Second Probate* issues with the Feds, then it might/may be okay to name the spouse a co-executor with the bank trust company. So be warned, that if you violate these rules and guidelines, you will have let the fox in the hen house. Then you end up not only probating your house, but your home.

These next several legal issues will seem complicated, but it really isn't so. Read it over several times, and you will soon get the picture to avoid a ticking time bomb within one's estate planning. Lawyers ignorant of these legal nuance areas have destroyed many estates, pension plans and family businesses, along with other glorious provisions referred to as **Prohibitive Transaction Rules under Public Law 93-406 and Code Section 4975.** So be cognizant that one has just got to love these two unnerving words "*prohibitive transactions,*" for they quickly disarm and set back on their heels the irritating lawyer or big accounting firm partner giving one grief. Ninety-nine percent of all lawyers and accountants know little if anything about, or understand issues about, "*prohibitive transaction,*" but it is a great finessing phrase for creating insecurity and inhibiting one's opposition. The knowledgeable use of the "*prohibitive transactions*" phrase can be the Goliath killer stone in one's sling even if bluffing too permanently or temporarily gain a debate team advantage. But I digress!

The subject at hand is **Code Section 318 > Attribution. Also referred to as the "Economic Community of Interest Doctrine"** This doctrine basically states that the Business Interest, Family Interest, Estate Interest, and Trust Interest can be merged and pyramided together as one interest. All these units can/may build on top of, and merge with each other if there are screw-up's to inflate the estate values for higher taxes, or sadly get some heirs disinherited.

This potential arena of grief, if one is not careful, has other identifying terminologies. They are referred to as **"Intra-family Dealings" and the "Unity of Ownership Doctrine."** So it is now time to review the attribution commonality chart:

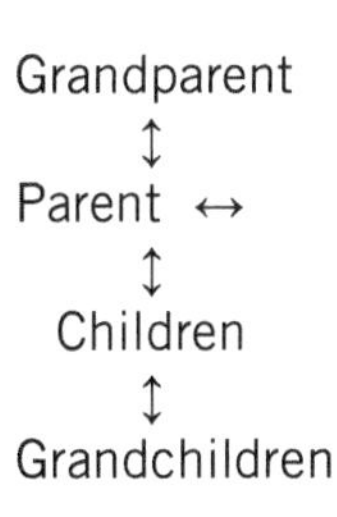

The liability and accountability issue will and can go backwards up from starting point ONE generation, and downwards TWO generations. Let's say it is stock in a family corporation the parent owns. Parent dies, everyone in this range may be penalized, and/or have all their stock redeemed back to the corporation.

Sadly, the sins a deceased person and his heirs usually pay for are most often surrounding the issues of asset valuations. The killer valuation problems most often deal with corporate stock valuations of a deceased person's percent of ownership and control interest. These premium control factors should have been identified and pegged down for estate purposes ahead of time, prior to one's death.

Note Code Section 2031-2F (2H) > This is the I.R.S clarification: "That you must set an established value on your assets before you die, or I.R.S. will establish its own values after you die." Now how clear can this section of law be?

One sure way to control this valuation is with a pegging agreement that is mandatory (not a first option or first right of refusal to purchase or redeem the stock). Next, use a set figure dollar amount, and not a formula to be determined later. The agreement must have a business purpose clause, and be supported with a professional independent appraisal. Then every year the owner(s) of the stock sit down and decide if the set-figure is still valid or needs to be changed. Afterwards, they sign and date the agreement again showing the up-dated annual review. The catch is to find a competent well trained attorney in this pegging valuation arena. Then get the process completed with an independent professional appraisal, and with proper legal documentation.

Now a word of caution on valuations: Do not play tricky games. **Know Code Sections 6659 (A Boot), 6651 (25% penalty), 6653 (plus a 5% negligence penalty)**, and don't think you're smarter than the courts and I.R.S. So, note a strange thing about valuations. That is, the WHOLE is one value, but the sum of the PARTS can be another value; particularly as to control issues pertaining to discounts, premiums, goodwill and other adjustments to the Fair Market Value. It is true that valuations are only a matter of opinion, but one is required by law to stabilize that opinion. So note this one particular case of record where a 1% common stock holder took on 40% of the valuation per the courts and I.R.S.

Take note, remember, and be weary if any lawyer, accountant, or other advisor attempts to pooh-pooh and belittle the previous information. Please ask the advisor this question; "How do you feel about tooth decay?" Then fire the advisor, for your estate does not want to become an I.R.S. test case to enrich everyone else but your intended heirs.

Here are some following rules and regulations for you to take note of, be aware of, and that you may need to do further research on at a later date. They will clearly (sort of) give you a clue, and speak for themselves

Code Section 2032A > Special Use Valuation: A mammoth and huge discount on estate valuations for only family farms and family businesses. The family must show and prove that they are not passive owners, and that they have more than a 50% active material participation with the farm or business.

Code Section 1.162 (a)(1) / (76 /9) > Unreasonable Compensation: What are the experiences and qualifications to allow a high level of compensation? Key around this issue is to have a two tier Compensation formula. A base salary plus bonus provision based upon sales, profits, or basic growth valuation of the business. * Violation penalties are stiff.*

Code Sections 482 *and* 269A > Reallocation of Income *and* Reconstruction of Income. Good Example of stupidity. A very successful do it all dentist in a rural farm land area, had the blessing of people who only paid in cash. He outright lied on his tax return about his income, and if the patient had 60/40 type of insurance coverage, he only showed the 60% number that the insurance company paid. Yet, he lived in a small mansion, drove only Mercedes 500's, and had a nice sailing yacht on Lake Erie. Then a disgruntled employee called I.R.S.; so here's proof that it only takes one to get you killed. And boy! Did this dentist pay a stiff price for being too shrewd?

Code Section 1.306-3 > The nasty penalizing "Tainted Stock Issue:" This can be suicide if you're a successful business corporation. But wait! Hidden within this nasty provision is a beautiful and fabulous loophole for a closely held family corporation to get potential tax benefits into with hundreds of thousands of dollars. You're wrong! will not be telling you what it is, for you need to ask your own corporate minute book keeping lawyer, and in particular the attorney who formed your new 1120-C corporation. Now if this lawyer does not know what you are talking about, and can not explain this great sheltered benefit to you; - Fire them!

So in the near slight conclusion of this section, **remember this key fact about S-corporations and L.L.C. - Corps.** That tax wise they are referred to as pass through corporations, - that are for beginners and losers. Now if your business is providing you the personal income you need, and now you have excess money to expand and reinvest in your business, or just want to accumulate some low taxed cash capital reserves; get the hell out of that S- corporation, and also switch to a Fiscal tax year like July $1^{st.}$ to June $30^{th.}$ the following year.

Then if any lawyer or accountant tells you otherwise: - Fire them! Their stupid and ignorant statement to you will be; "You do not want to be a C-Corp. because you will pay a double tax." With this type of displayed ignorance, - double fire them!

We need to return back to the "Time Warp" again; since you have been shown the Check Mate information to block legal and accounting advisors from leading you like a lamb to the slaughter. Advisors too often rely on one's ignorance to slaughter the estate, and dilute wealth and success to earn unjustified profits. Therefore, remember it is never too late, and you're never too young or old to face reality. The fact is, one does not get younger or healthier, but in time only gets slower, sicker and older. According to the Wall Street Journal, we all learned that mortality sooner or later is 100%. Also, when the big eraser comes down out of the sky, and your body goes to room temperature; you're no longer with us in this world.

So we now time warp back about 300 years to capture the great words of a Japanese samurai / Yamamoto Tsuneetomo:

> "Whether people be of high or low birth, rich or poor, old or young, enlightened or confused, they are all alike in that they will one day die. It is not that we don't know that we will die some day, but we grasp at straws.
>
> While knowing that we will die some day, we think that all the others will die before us, and that we will be the last to go. Death seems to be a long way off. Is this not shallow thinking? It is worthless, and is only a joke within a dream. It will not do to think in such a way and be negligent. Insofar as death is always at one's door, one should make sufficient effort and act quickly to protect and preserve what one cherishes."

Wow! - What up-to-date thinking, and for all those struggling for success, one must remember that the "Future is no longer what it used to be, and it will take all the running you can do, just to stay in the same place." That is why this chapter is designed to allow you to stay in the game, and defeat your block and tackle opposition. But in doing so, just remember that shrouds do not have pockets.

This is why, as a business owner while living in the moment, and striving in the moment to maintain or gain success; - there are in this time warp future relative issues and needs one must be aware of for comfortable continuation or liquidation of one's success. As previously mentioned, people actively plan for going into business, but often too late consider needed plans for going out of business due to death, disability, retirement, or just a good merger or sale business offer. So when the peddle meets the metal of KEEP vs. SELL as related to business or farm operations, one had better remember Section 2031-2F, Section 318, and other issues as goodwill and non-compete clauses, and value discounts or premium factoring for tax profit and tax benefits. Thus remember, that valuation is really a matter of opinion, so one must try to stabilize that opinion in advance to capitalize upon opportunity, or to avoid negative legal and taxing adversity when things go helter-skelter.

There is an Old Russian story you need to remember, and best to hear again. It was freezing winter weather. A Russian potato farmer carrying a heavy bag of potatoes was treading back from the potato field to his home, and he was freezing. He heard this small bird chirping for help, and it was on the ground near frozen to death.

The farmer picked it up and held it in his hands to warm the bird up. But could not keep doing so, or his hands would freeze. He could not hold both the bird and the heavy bag of potatoes. He noticed some fresh warm moose dropping, and made a hole in the middle of the warm moose dropping. The farmer put the little bird down in the warm moose dropping, and went on this way. Now the bird was warm and recovering, and started chirping loudly with joy. A wolf heard the bird. The wolf was hungry and went up and bites the bird right out of the moose crap and ate it.

The moral of the story is: The one who put you in it may not be your enemy, and the one who took you out of it, may well not be your friend.

It is fitting that you are now introduced to one of the more dangerous words in law that can get you and your family killed by the government and I.R.S. The word is applied to people who think they are smarter than the system, and that they may be getting away with something under the table or behind the barn.

That word is "CONSTRUCTIVE;"- so you must now fill in the blank spaces:

If it walks like a ____, quacks like a ____, maybe looks like a ____: It is a ____ (Pig acting like a duck?!?!).

Now is when one tried to convince the hangman they're a goose, swan, donkey or goat, but to no avail. **They see only** > Constructive Receipt (1.451-2a), Constructive Transfer (Sec. 2038), Constructive Dividend, Constructive (imputed) interest, Constructive Acts Between The Parties, Constructive Partnership / Agreements, Constructive viewed Income Compensation as excess earning, unreasonable earnings, excess accumulated earnings. Constructive Marriage (Cohabitation, 1 year / 1 day -plus); > this really raises hell with Pre-Marital Agreement, because they left out the word "Post." - Constructive Intra-family dealings, the Active role and participant test, Control Group / Brother-Sister Corporate Group issues, and Section 2036. These are the real great gotcha areas at law.

<u>Now we conclude with the extremely important subject of real estate titling</u>: . . .

First, if one is a widow, widower, single and has an Intervivos Trust (A living trust), then the Real Estate should be titled in their name-trustee. Otherwise it is just titled in their name, and disposed of per provisions of the will with probate. Now note three other types of titling; one not so good, and two are excellent. First, the not so good deed will be covered, but it is one of the big mistakes married couples make and/or family members.

Tenancy in Common: > Most often properly used between business partners where there are two, three, four or more co-owners in the real estate. Each one's will control their %-age interest, or they have a buy and sell agreement between themselves. This is a probate deed, and married couples should never have this deed. Yet the majority of married couples do out of ignorance and bad advice. Plus, the deed provides no form of creditor protection.

Joint Tenancy with Rights of Survivorship: > many times referred to as the <u>*AND/OR*</u> deed. Avoids probate, but provides absolutely no creditor protection. Often used between spouses, okay! But best used with a non-spouse family member that you wish to inherit the real estate. It can be <u>used only</u> with one child (one only, not two or three on the deed). The single parent and child are considered equal co-owners, and either one can dissolve the tenancy without the other's approval. Title then reverts back to Tenancy in Common.

Estate (Tenancy) by the Entireties: > the gold mine deed. The number one best deed between a husband and wife. Both spouses have title to the whole, 100% zero probate w/ immediate transfer of the whole interest upon death to the surviving spouse. Plus, individual creators cannot lien the property, for it has full creditor protection. Note, this is the best deed if spouse is a non-citizen resident alien.

We now close with the last words of advice. The first is to make sure your family knows whether you want to be cremated (burned), or have a regular common burial (wormed). Now this may really sound stupid, but make absolutely sure in writing which spouse the deceased person is to be buried with. A real potential lawsuit problem may occur with extended families, with multiple spouses, and different children with different marriages, or whatever?!?!

And a last point: Please! Please! Do not place a major written Bio. history about the deceased person in the obituary column. Here is where you then tell the whole world of crooks and con men the time and place of the memorial and funeral services. Don't be ignorant enough to give the history of the family with dates; times, places, ages, military service, lodges and associations belonged to, and full names of children, grandchildren and other relatives with address locations. Wow! Gold mine of info for the evil doers.

The final related comment here is, do not, never-never bury valuables and jewelry with the deceased in the casket. One can guarantee you that it will never-never get in the ground. Fact is, that many undertakers and lawyers have gotten rich on buried treasure. The other opportunity for buried treasure in rural areas is when the first people in the deceased person's home after death are the undertaker and/or lawyer. Their first in-house home inspections have discovered great China Collections, Shot Gun Collections, Antique Furniture, Art works, and much more. Wow! All these wonderful items the lawyer or undertaker gets to add to their own private museums at no cost; all these vanishing assets are unbeknownst to the expectant ignorant heirs?!?!

One case is quite humorous. When the grieving family returned home after the funeral, plus a dedication memorial service, and a special luncheon at the country club; they get a surprise only to find, - Guess what? Their house was totally empty. The crooks from the newspaper Obit notice knew the family and neighbors would be gone for hours. So they came by with a moving van, and moved all the home item assets without the family's awareness that they had even hired a mover.

There are many incidences where homes have been robbed during funeral services. There have been tons of incidences where relatives have been conned and ripped off based upon the connecting of personal information in the obituary columns. So while one is fast becoming cynical about the living, it has unexpectedly flipped open a Pandora's box of troubles as related to the dying.

Yet there are only two things that bother me about the obituary columns. <u>**One,**</u> it shows that all the people are dying in alphabetical order, and my first last name initial is "D." Second, why are they always smiling and looking so pleasant? For by their pictures most died so young and youthful looking with the possibility of a long, long life ahead of them.

At the time of one's birth, and as one proceeds up the road towards success; remember that you started building a mortgage that the I.R.S. will call in within nine months or there abouts. This unpaid mortgage is referred to as Federal Estate Taxes, but also be aware that many states have high state inheritance taxes. For while you are living and working, the I.R.S. collects the interest, - and upon one's death, they call in the principal. So if you're a person of wealth with little liquidity, this sudden call for cash upon death will be the kiss of death upon one's family heirs. For the reality is that the I.R.S. only wants cash, and not property.

So in closing this chapter, the hope is that one has gained a real awareness of preventive legality factors, and has been granted the wisdom and insight to avoid those Plato lawyers. The ones practicing "Dental Law:" Where a dentist always leaves in under that new filling, a little tooth decay; so the dentist will get more profitable dental work later. This practice is referred to as a Houdini Clauses in legal work; like leaving out the important Business Continuity Clause in one's estate documents, or the word Post in a Pre-Marital Agreement. For here is where the lawyers win by vulturine tactics in the game of Finders Keepers.

As Plato said; "Those small unrighteous soul's of lawyers;"- or as mentioned in Luke 11:46-52. Today they are known for the behind your back practice of "Proctology Law," and even worse "Hysterectomy Law," where they rob one of their first born. Many are 'Ghost Attorneys' hiding behind an Annuity Salesman, a Pension Service firm, or an Investment Firm.

Many of these lawyers have been disbarred or have resigned from the bar in another state, moved south or west, and then say they are a "Federally Licensed Attorney" to get some phony credibility. Real Skull and Bones! .

So always be aware, be prepared, and learn your lessons well. For lest thee not forget; **"For want of a nail. . ."** Now close your eyes, and use the imagination to paint a graphic picture in the mind as relating to the following story about two angry farmers fighting over a beautiful Holstein milk cow.

The one farmer was yelling and pulling on the cow's tail, and the other farmer was yelling and pulling on the cows' horns. While this was going on, a lawyer was sitting on a milk stool by the cows utter, milking the cow for all it was worth.

#

CHAPTER VI

Tomorrow can be today's future:

[Several key sample forms for self preservation, plus a few legal terms and regulations to know.]

Let us start off with a couple of nice illustrative stories to make the points necessary for understanding the inner-workings for success: . . .

There was this young person struggling for achievement in this life, and getting a little frustrated. Then one night, this person had a dream that they came upon the great storehouse where God keeps the marvelous gifts that he bestows on mankind. The warehouse was guarded by an Angel, with a huge sign above the door stating; "Fruits of Mankind."

This individual said to the Angel in charge; "I am so tired of the miseries of life on earth! Instead of wars and afflictions, lust and lies, we need love and joy, peace and justice. So please give me some of these things." The Angel smiled and answered; "We do not stock fruits, only the seeds."

The story reminds one of the song verses that start off with; "Is that all there is; is that all there is my friend, is that all there is..." Makes one wonder why people can't act differently without knowing; rather than too often saying after the fact, "If I had only known." Guess the old saying is factual; "Every person has a blind spot, a blank in their vision of life and others, and one is lucky if they only have one." Many just give up with, "It is what it is!" Hope not!

Isn't it amazing how few people can see beyond their own eyes, and then they tend to have no vision. When this happens, they begin to parish with a slow death of indifference. Robert Burns put it nicely; "It is too bad we can not see ourselves as others see us." Yes, this would be a real blind spot, for blocking one's success. There was this blind inspirational speaker who really made one think about this statement; "If you could only see what I hear." Interesting?!?!

Now for a tidbit story concerning a rabbit and a squirrel. The rabbit played all summer and fall without a care in the world. The squirrel worked and stored up food for the winter. Now in the late fall the rabbit came to the squirrel crying and complaining that he had nothing to eat for the winter, and asked the squirrel to share. The squirrel answered; "You danced around all summer long thinking you're going to get a job in Hollywood." The squirrel paused a second and said; "Well, I know of a place where there are some of last year's nuts, and there is an entrance."

The rabbit went to the place, but the entrance hole was too small. The hole was only for the size of a mouse. Now the rabbit got all upset, and said to the squirrel; "I'd have to be the size of a mouse to get the food, and how could I do that?" The squirrel's response, "I gave you the answer; you have to work out the details." So sad; the rabbit was more concerned about the comforts and pleasures of the moment, and forgot about the essential and important things in life. The same goes for many individuals where life just passes them by, or maybe they just passed by life? The clear fact is that one becomes what they commit themselves to; for weakness today, enslaves us tomorrow. It is never what you say that counts, but what you do.

The major part of becoming successful is learning how to ask the right questions at the right time, and then when to shut your mouth and listen. It is always amazing how many people do not listen, and worse yet, do not want to hear the answer after asking the question. One can always spot these ignorant souls, for they do not and did not know the answer themselves, but will argue about the validity of the proper answer.

It is always best to let people like this die in their own ignorance, for they are their own worst enemy. This is also why one must learn early in life to dump and walk away from wasteful and useless friendships, and even from nice relatives before being drawn down to their level of selfishness and/or self-centered fantasy world. Note the belief concepts that "blood is thicker than water," and that "love conquers all." All crap!! This thinking in reality, sooner or later, and quite often sooner, will get one killed while traveling down "The yellow brick road" toward success. Yet this is all part of one paying their dues as a hardcore learning experience, as going along that other so-called road; - "That road to hell, too often paved with good intentions."

Now, what an appropriate time to mention: ***"The Innocent Spouse Rule."*** This is the one rule that can save many an ex-spouse after a divorce, many a heartache and tears, and let one know that their divorce lawyer was most likely a money making incompetent. The sad joke is, that it is usually women who get pillaged and plundered the most, and too often by lawyer's oversight and negligence.

Fact is, every ex-spouse within twelve months from the time a divorce is final should complete Government Form 8577. Then give notice to every Tom, Dick and Harry to avoid liability as to unknown and potential problems from the ex-spouse's business, financial, and legal activity. Those sins and omissions not realized or known about that could come surprising out of nowhere concerning the past secretive or conniving ex-spouse's actions. Also a sad fact, but often so true, is that many loving spouses do not always protect the financial integrity of their loving mate while still married.

Now the following clearly proves the "Test of the Greater Fool Theory," and why many single people, young and old, should note and pay attention to some of Judge Judy's T.V. shows. Then ignorant individuals would soon learn the meaning of building a Chinese wall, and that it is "better to be safe than sorry." Neglect in the following area has caused many a legal action, and has gotten deserving heirs shafted.

Note: ***"A public recognition of a mutual co-habitation."*** This is one area where people keep living in yesterday, and forget that the world keeps going around. They hang onto old thinking and ideas that are no longer valid on the books. Here is where old legal concepts have long since been changed by court decisions and sharp attorney presentations. Yet, three states are thought not to recognize co-habitation agreements, stating that it violates God's law. These states are Illinois, Georgia and Louisiana, but this could change overnight by a judge's ruling on a well presented case.

Okay!! You prefer to rely on some state's old obsolete Common Law Marriage Rules; that's fine. You may later enjoy becoming an expensive test case when all could have been avoided with a simple sample type; agreement as follows.

MUTUAL Memorandum of Understanding and Wishes:

Between. . .

________________ & ________________

Both parties to this agreement desire to waive all Rights and Privileges under Domestic Relations Law, Marital Rights Law, and Mutual Cohabitation issues at law as to their past, present, and future relationships.

Both parties understand the relationship is based upon a mutual friendship and trust between said parties. Assets known to be part of, or titled to each party's ownership rights or estate considerations (tangible or intangible), are considered separate and independently distinct from the other party's interest and claims, or even the other party's heirs.

Any agreed to mutual exception or exemptions that the parties' desire, due to the nature of their friendship, are listed as follows, and restricted only to those specific items and conditions listed; ...

1. ________________________________
2. ________________________________
3. ________________________________

Both named parties agree not to claim any inheritance rights to the assets of the other party's estate, and have no claim to income sources of the other party to this specific agreement. - - - The final statement of simplicity is that, what is mine is mine, what is theirs is theirs, and neither the twine shall meet as to any form of legal or equitable fee, or life interest rights to the parties of the agreement or to their heirs.

***** [Both sign, date, have two independent witnesses, and have their signatures properly notarized.] *****

This Co-habitation concept apparently has a new twist for achieving a reverse benefit as follows. This high income professional was paying his ex-spouse $8,000.00 per month in alimony. Then Oop's! His ex-spouse was found to be apparently living with someone in a status of Public Recognition of a Mutual Co-habitation. This professional man hired a private detective who did his homework extremely well. The detective obtained an abundance of evidence along with solid testimony that his ex-wife and new lover boyfriend were indeed in an established recognized co-habitation state for over 21 months. **Wow!!** No more $8,000.00 per month alimony. ***Why?*** The ignorant lovers did not have a signed and executed Co-habitation agreement.

Now we're entering the arena where one with nothing to lose, takes on the one with a lot to lose. The arguments for the nothing to lose side are that it is against their religion, or it will taint their real true love and affection for each other. Bull!! These statements are a con game piece of bull crap, for if both parties in the arena are ethical with honest good intentions; everyone wins in the long run with nothing to lose. Here is where one in sound mind and body has now achieved financial success, and has their protective brain in gear; will acquire and purchase a fair disability insurance policy against the possibility of divorce ***or a*** *premature death (nasty extended family heirs?).* The safety net policy is referred to as **a "Pre** ***and*** **'Post' Marital Agreement."**

Think about it? Having a pre/post nuptial is like putting on a seatbelt when driving your car. You don't click it on because you are expecting to have an accident. It is only for protection should you have an accident. Maybe a humorist point might twinkle the thought button. The surviving spouse was at the lawyer's office, and the lawyer said; "Your husband left you all of his wealth and fortune." The widow asked, "What does that mean?" The lawyer's response was; "Means that you are now a much more attractive women than you were last week."

Please do not be coerced with phony passion into a marriage with someone whose primary objective is financial security. True it could be only for social convenience and prestige, or they are looking to hook onto a nurse and a purse. Either way, they win even if you don't die. They still have the option of winning by getting a one-half plus settlement with a costly and nasty divorce. So the prenup discussion is one good way to separate the wheat from the chaff, or the Wana-be's from the Really-be's. To find a good attorney call: 1-800-ESQUIRE.

Sad part is, most pre/post nuptials are voided out, not for agreement errors, but by ignorant acts performed by those involved. Yet, most of the time it is a failure to inform on the part of the lawyer. **Such as** . . .

- Full & Fair disclosure in writing of all assets and their values provided to each party prior to signing their agreement and marriage, and in the future no merging of assets.
- Separate Attorney representing each person's interest to the signing of the agreement with their written opinions and review prior to marriage.
- Agreement must not be signed under duress or undue influence; such as being pregnant, signed only a day or two before the wedding, or the last minute on the chapel steps. Oh yes! Must be in sound mind and body, and not intoxicated or high on brownies at the time.
- No evidence of collusion, fraudulent intent, willful deception, or conflicting subterfuge with wills and trusts; and please, not later after an event born child. Advice to all males; always get a vasectomy first, for very obvious and good reason {Called infidelity with an old boyfriend or ex-husband.}. Particularly if said male is age 58, and the new bride to be actuarial chick is age 36. It is the wallet?!?!
- Do not ever, never give spouse business or financial power of attorney, or have them sign on as a signature guarantee. Do not have them as Secretary of the corporation, and never, never file a joint tax return, - PERIOD!
- Now to be fair, as often stated; "One who marries for money will end up earning every damn dime of it. Particularly when the age 38 becomes 58, and the age 58 spouse is now baggage at age 78.

There is no attempt here for overkill on the Cohabitation and Prenuptial agreement issues. But they are always needed when the wonderful companion has a "Prozac rebound," and becomes a Jeckel and Hyde. That is when the lovely 'glass slipper of love' becomes a Combat Boot.

Now God forbid that one should become deceased, for then it is hopeful that the person properly protected and provided for a spouse, family, or other potential heirs. The why is, the deceased's estate enters into a state of accountable probate, and hopefully only into one state of probate. It is an irreconcilable fact that probate has received a bad rap, but most of this bad rap was in the past, even in the past century, and misplaced by a lot of false propaganda today by Annuity Sales people, and "five and dime" legal people.

There are basically only four reasons estates have probate problems that can create unjust enrichment for you know who.

1. Person dies intestate with no will. Then only the lawyer capitalizes or cannibalizes upon the error with delays, and then gains convenient profitable benefits. But sadly, people blame the probate court process, not the negligent and ignorant deceased, or the "wolf in sheep's clothing."
2. Greedy, incompetent, self-serving, and/or unethical lawyers. They draw documents with Houdini Clauses and open end trap doors. Two well known probate judges, one in Columbus, Ohio and the other in Brooklyn, N.Y, have said it best; "Dead people get little or no respect when money and valuable assets gets involved".

   As a lawyer once said; "Why complain about our fees, for they are now dead, and their cash needs are so small." This is a matter of record; that a known so-called reputable attorney settled a $2,200,000.00 estate with proper documents, but all the heirs lived out of the state. The lawyer's approved rip-off fee charged to the estate was $600,000.00.
3. Federal Estate #706 probate filing: People of substance and means with large estates over five million dollars, or maybe even three and a half million dollars later down the road, actually have two probates.

   <u>First</u>, the local harmless probate (except for the lawyers). Then the following second stage #706 probate with I.R.S. along with real lawyer and accountant complications. Yet, take note that many states still have rather high state inheritance taxes with rather low exemptions that are far below the federal estate tax exemption.
4. Internal family ignorance, screw-ups and oversights as to Attribution issues, Valuation issues, Life Insurance issues, extended family issues, and those greedy self-interest combative heirs. There is often a lot of negative apprehension between an estate being wisely handled while being distributed *<u>equitably.</u>* or questionably handled *<u>as equal</u>* with cold distributions between the heirs that may or may not be fair, or reasonable.

One just has to love a former Franklin County Probate Judge in Columbus Ohio. He would post the names on the Court House door of the abusive lawyers who were improperly screwing around with people's estates. He then demanded lawyers get a lot of documented continuing education in estate issues, or they could not practice in his court. One just had to admire this Judge Metcalf.

So note the following guidelines; for soon it will become apparent, if you get rid of and side step the freelance lawyer's role then you're home free when considering the following information, and with a sample guidance form for the competent estate attorney to assist one and/or the family. But first the sample general form to guide a competent attorney:

Attorney: Date:

________ **Reciprocal Wills** ______

and/or

Intervivos Trust *with*

[Catch All Pour-over will]

__ Self-Declaratory / A-B Trust

[Credit Shelter B - - __ Full __ Limited]

- - OR - -

**** Only simple will(s) with possibly a contingent trust, w/ Bank Trust Co. as sole Executor or as a Co-Executor with selected individual. ****

___ Multiple Power Liquidity insurance trust:

___ Beneficiary Controlled Trust:

___ Q-tip (Fee Estate) / Qualified Terminal Interest provision:

___ Special Needs Trust for impaired person:

___ Memorandum of Trust

**** Springing Power of Attorney, Financial Power of Atty., Health Proxy Power of Atty., Living Will, D.N.R. [Do not resuscitate order.]****

*** Now list the full legal names, dates of birth, and Social Security numbers of all family members; -plus complete legal addresses of residency.**

*** Also list any other persons that may be classified as a beneficiary. And state if spouse or others are U.S. Citizen or a Resident Alien:**

*** Business interest involved, provide full business name, Federal I.D. #, and complete addresses; plus estimated value, type of business entity, and whether fiscal or calendar accounting year.**

1. Executor/Personal Rep. > Bank Trust / __________
2. Trustee: First Self; Second Bank Trustee ___________
3. Advisor to trust > 1st. Spouse, 2nd. _______________
4. Advisor w/ power to fire trustee / select new Bank Trustee.
5. No Bonding, — Per Stirpes, — Alienation Clause on heirs.
6. Provide <u>multiple</u> Alternate Guardians (of persons, not property) where needed, and do so with extrinsic writing, so easier to change down the road. ** [If doctor, may also need a medical business guardianship, for privilege information dies with the doctor.]:
7. Ninety day Common Disaster Clause. > <u>But</u> w/ a Marital Trust, waive the common disaster clause.
8. ***Special note:*** **No** limited Power of Appointment or Hanging Powers, **&** avoid violation of Reciprocal Trust Doctrine; ***<u>plus</u>*** note any needed E.P.A. waiver issues.
9. *<u>Business Continuity Clause</u>* if applicable - in the will (A MUST):
10. <u>Special</u> <u>bequest</u>**?** > Elderly Parents (Income only)
    Per Capita/ brothers or sisters
    ** <u>Generation</u> <u>Skipping</u> <u>Trust</u>
11. Gunslinger disinheritance clause for anyone who challenges the will or trust is disinherited; their trust or will allocation reduced to Zero, or at least a minimum $1,000.00.
12. Final disposition if all killed with no surviving issue; where? [So assets do not revert back to the state, better to a charity.]
13. Want to disinherit an individual? Still name them in the will, but give them a nominal amount of money, like $1000.00.

Shows you did not forget them, and also did not outright insult them. Helps avoid legal issues.

14. Check all Life Insurance policies to make sure no violation of Section 2042 -> "Incidents of Ownership." ***Also,*** be sure all pension, 401K and IRA beneficiary forms are correct. [Can not disinherit a spouse (1st./2nd./ or 3rd.) by using a Pension/401K beneficiary designation.]
15. Two (2) notarized witness affidavit statements; - Plus sign every page of the will and trust on bottom right.

By now, one should realize that the majority of probate problems are not caused by I.R.S., or the local Courts. Most of the caused problems, by the real culprits, have already been explained along with "Ignorance of the law is no excuse." So the real world ballgame as to estates and probate has radically changed for ninety-eight percent of all estates since they will no longer be dealing with the #706 Federal Estate tax probate issues. Since no longer dealing, *for the time being*, with very low Federal Estate exemptions of *$600,-Thousand*, or $*1,-Million*, $2,-*Million*, or even $3.5-Million.

Now for estates under the Federal exemption: No real problems as long as one has a Chinese wall to block out the Big Bad Wolf. That magic wall is naming a Bank Trust Company as the sole Executor or Co-Executor as mentioned before. Trust Company does the job for 1.4% to 2%, but I've never heard of any attorney assisting for less that 5% to 8%, and that's if they have some integrity. **So if . . .**

- No minor / immature children under age 25 / no mentally or physically impaired children; 'after both parents deceased.'
- Single, widow, widower parent; - or remarried with solid Prenuptial or a good Co-habitation agreement.
- No need for a Q-tip (Life Estate) provision for the surviving spouse, if you feel the surviving spouse is capable, competent, and trusted.
- Executor / Administrator is Bank Trust Company; not ever a private trust company, nor any financial or legal advisor.

- If applicable: Business Continuity Clause in the Will.

So a proper solution is quite simple and less expensive, by . . .

1. Reciprocal Wills w/ 90 day Common Disaster Clause. If you're single, a will w/ same; but if you need a trust for some reason, just have a contingent testamentary trust on death.
2. Estate by (Tenancy)Entireties Deed w/ Spouse, OR "Guy A *and/or* Person B Survivorship"- use only with one non-spousal person.
3. Joint & Survivor Ownership Declaration for all non-titled assets. *Do it yourself* —> and notarized with two witnesses.
4. Letter of Wishes —> Burned or Wormed? Who gets that particular ring, or antique furniture, or artwork? Also notarized with two witnesses. *Do it yourself.*
5. Springing Durable Power of Atty. + Healthy Proxy Power of Atty. + Financial Power of Atty. + a Living Will (Pull the plug), and?!?! D.N.R. order?!?!

Let's face it: 5% to 8% plus extraordinary charges and expenses is a lot of real money to settle one's estate in probate. So if one's deceased estate would be a net million dollars the lawyer would earn $50,-thousand to $80,-thousand dollars *plus* for a part time job over a couple months; let's say on the outside four to six months max. Now please realize, this is assuming one's estate size is under any State Inheritance Tax level *and/or* under and within the Federal #706 Estate Tax exemption level. Now should one's larger estate fall into these death tax areas, then pay 1.4% to 2% to a Bank Trust Company as executor to the estate for the surviving spouse or family heirs. It should be obvious that 2% is far less than 5% or 8% *plus*.

Truth be known, why shouldn't the spouse or key heirs take on a learning experience part time job themselves for a couple months and earn $50,000.00 to $80,000.00 plus (equivalent to having a nice tax free income)?

Now if one has an I.Q. higher than a tulip with some degree of educational intelligence, can read and write, follow simple direction, and know their multiplication tables; ONE CAN DO THE PROBATE PROCESS THEMSELVES. THEN KEEP THE VALUABLE MONEY

TO THEMSELVES for a little part time effort, with plenty of nice help if needed at the probate clerk's office.

Please consider the following directions. First locate the will, and identify the executor named in the will. Then collect many copies of the Death Certificate, for they will be needed to collect insurance, transfer titling of assets, collect on pensions and I.R.A.'s, and other requested needs for verification purposes. Next INVENTORY all assets with stated and/or appraised values as of the Date of Death time period (Bank and Brokerage accounts, property values [Real Estate and Personal Assets], insurance policies death benefit values, and pension paid out values; - Etc.

NOW take all this organized information with a death certificate and copy of the will <u>and/or</u> separate living trust to the County Court House and <u>file</u> <u>only</u> the will part with the County Clerk within thirty (30) days of the date of death. ***<u>Special note:</u>*** The probate clerk does not in any way ever keep a copy of the trust; - they only keep a copy of the will. The separate living trust provisions are private and confidential, and only shown for verification that it has valid existence for holding other non-probated undisclosed private assets.

<u>Next,</u> pay all of the bills and debts, such as utilities, funeral costs, medical bills, mortgage, and leases. Also send notice of death to all creditors. Now the creditors have 90 days to submit claims to the estate for payment. Then terminate leases, credit cards, magazines, notify banks, government agencies (Soc. Sec. /Veterans Etc.), Post Office, and notify credit reporting companies as Equifax, TransUnion and Experian. In the meantime notify all beneficiaries that they are beneficiaries, but <u>ONLY</u> distribute to them <u>LAST</u> after the estate is cleaned up and near finalized.

With all now said and done, one must prepare and file a final tax return, with the accountant's assistance. Please take note that in most state jurisdictions, <u>net</u> estates under $200,000.00 (Plus or minus) are classified as no administration. Simple; file all with probate clerk, pay a small fee, and go home. Now for <u>net</u> estates over $200,000.00 (Plus or minus), there is required court supervision, but this is not a really difficult issue, and you may get to meet the nice judge. Wow!! One did this heart rending part-time job all on their own, and kept in their pocket a savings of <u>5%</u> or <u>8%</u> (*<u>plus</u>* ordinary charges and expenses) for themselves and their heirs. Plus, it kept them busy without moping and depressing themselves sitting at home alone bored and frustrated.

By now it should be obvious to all, that you, your family and heirs are not to be the Productive Goose that laid the Golden Eggs for someone else's benefit. So we are back at the beginning with the keys for prevailing being first knowledge, learning from one's experiences, developing unique people skills, and knowing the right questions to ask; *Oh yes!!* - & > C.Y.A. But there was this musical play "Chicago" where this individual was complaining about all the advisors, particularly the lawyer. The complaint was that the advisors only saw this person as Mister Cellophane, and that they never saw him; -"They only see through me, only walk by me." Oh how true this often is in life.

Yet, Atticus Finch in "To Kill a Mockingbird" made a related comment with merit; "You never know someone until you step inside their skin, and walk around a little." But in life one must also learn to live within their own skin, and that becomes Utopia. Therefore, the following stories should make an impression for thought about one's future success.

The training in India for control and handling of elephants involves locking an ankle bracelet with a heavy chain onto the elephant's leg. Then trainers hook the other end of the heavy chain to a very large tree. The elephant fights, struggles and strains for several weeks trying to break away from the anchored down status to the big tree trunk. Finally after several weeks of suffering the elephant finally gives up and lays down, and now the elephant becomes totally manageable by their trainer.

The trainer now releases the one end of the chain from the large tree, but leaves the heavy chain and ankle bracket on the elephant's leg. Now the trainer hooks the other end of the elephant's restrainer chain to a small stake driven into the ground. But now the elephant is so conditioned at being restrained, that it does not even realize it can rip the small stake out of the ground, raise a little hell, and take a hike. So my question will always be to you; "What small stake is holding you back from success in this life?"

Now for a true story about George Bernard Shaw. A very elite British Literary Guild had several over egoist snob writers who did not appreciate that George Bernard Shaw was accepted as a member. They felt he was a little on the uncouth side, and below their social status intellectually and knowledge wise as to his literary skill.

Several of the upscale jerks decided to try and embarrass Mr. Shaw in front of the other society members. They bragged to others about the stunt to shame Mr. Shaw, with a trick question, once he arrived at the private club's formal guild meeting; the snobs called Mr. Shaw up to the front of the room, and said; "Did you know George, that there are only three words in the English language that start with "Su-? They are Summit, Sumac, and Sugar." George Bernard Shaw thought for a minute, and said "Sure!"

The following graph is interesting since cash in business and in life generally means security and success if properly earned, and managed well.

Today the word <u>CASH</u> needs to be looked at a bit deeper; . . .

C.— confidence > (comes with knowledge):
A.— attitude > (positives attract):
S. — system > (idea? -> try it!!):
H.— help > (Serve First!):

Now what does it take for one to know their future wealth if they invest the same dollar amount every year. The following multipliers are at 5%, the other at 8% if these were based upon an annual set savings amount each year, and the annual return on that savings each year thereafter for the total accumulated values.

	5 yrs. /	10 yrs. /	15 yrs. /	25 yrs.
Amount @ 5% X	5.802	13.207	22.657	50.113
[?}				
Amount @ 8% X	6.336	15.645	29.234	78.954
[?}				

This makes it clear that disciplined savings can amount to a lot of security dollars down the road in one's future.

Since we've had a respite on seriousness, we must go back to seriousness. I feel it is now necessary to point out that there is something far worse than death and the lack of sufficient funds for retirement. That is the dungeon of despair where lawyers benefit from their "Full Employment Relief Act," known as the Guardianship Court. The Guardianship Court is very expensive, and has all the charm and grace of being in a Greyhound Bus Station on a Saturday night. Yet, conservancy and guardianship is manageable as long as law firms do not get the management authority, and the wise family members have pre-planned with proper documentation.

Disability is one area where family members must avoid the Christmas syndrome. Where they see no evil, hear no evil, and refuse to admit facts to themselves until it often becomes too late; particularly during the early stages of a long term progressive degenerative illness. So early on, admit the illness and have a full family meeting A.S.A.P. Then inventory all family resources, have proper legal documents for authoritative actions, learn all about the illness, locate all community care and support groups, and get signature control over all assets. Also redo wills, and change life insurance and pension beneficiaries so that the disabled person is not an Oop's! Beneficiary.

Take these words of wisdom to heart; guardianship court is no place to be, and care giving is a physical and mental drain on a spouse and/or family members. Sadly, but way too often, the Coup d'état will be within the County or Municipal Guardianship Court where they appoint a legal representative. You can believe this as fact; it is terrible being father to your father, or mother to your mother. Also, one can not wait until the last moment to put legal affairs in order, for the Government has a Five (5) year look back to reverse taken actions not to their benefit (Like in the areas of gifting and transferring of assets.).

Yes, it may be someone else's squirrelly thinking that gives you the answers, but only you can start hopping around to work out the details. So remember that it was Humpty Dumpty who sat on the wall, and it was Humpty Dumpty who had the great fall. Yet all the King's horses and all the King's men could not put poor Humpty Dumpty back together again. Actually, no relative should trust all the King's men to change a light bulb, let alone take care of their parents, or the first born. So the key for self preservation and peace of mind is only based upon one's own knowledge, plus hard work to obtain financial security, psychic income, and a hopeful caring and loving family life. It may well be as you wish it for tomorrow, but a burdensome tomorrow needs money first and foremost. Since love and patience can be strained to the breaking point without thought and preparation.

So what is the great outlook picture for tomorrow's economics, based upon a current snap shot of this present moment in time? One key overused and mis-described word is "uncertainty." This word puts fear in the hearts of the ignorant and turns their brains to jelly. Okay! This same shot in the dark word was used in the yesterdays, today, and will be overused for all tomorrows. Yet it will make the knowledgeable wise person financially successful and secure.

Therefore, one needs to stand back and take a broad view observation that creates great opportunities for success. Macro to Micro 101 Economics:

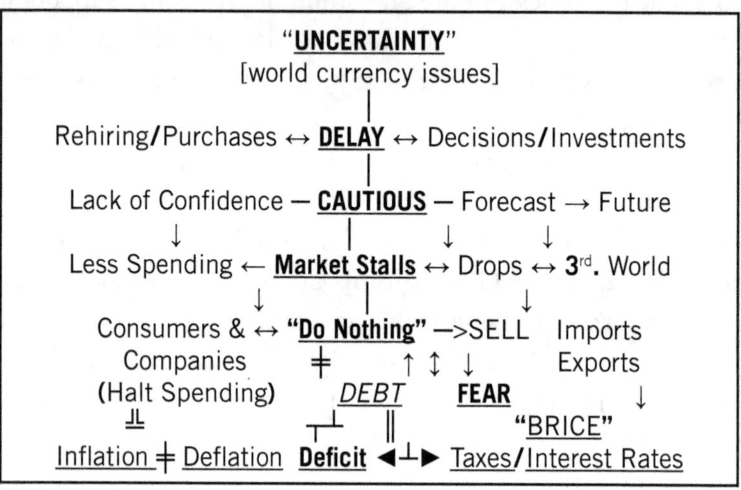

Yeah! Seems a little complicated, but it is well structured. But as a physics Professor once said; "There is no such thing as gravity, the world sucks." But this may well not be so if one has a well structured and designed plan with the near perfect twenty-five (25/75) seventy-five solution. The following will break down this principle as a working guideline regardless of one's family income. So at the beginning, before any type of structured planning, one is required first to pay their taxes. Next they need to spend on maintaining their standard of living, but way too often the last thing people adequately do is save their money for the future. This must change and be reversed.

The key for financial security, peace of mind, and a decent retirement is based upon one's self-discipline to Save First. Next, is to Maintain one's Standard of Living, and LAST with proper planning is to pay fewer taxes.

- **Now** for the 25% non-discretionary savings part;
  DEATH -> Life Insurance & Social Security cost.
  DISABILITY -> Insurance cost for Medical, Hospital, & Income protection, ***plus*** Social Security.
  RETIREMENT -> IRA, 401K, Profit Sharing, Pension.
  ** ***Plus*** one's own Social Security.

Now these three (3) points are the solid rock pillars for success. These pillars protect and support one's current and future Standard of Living from sinking upon a weak foundation of quicksand.

- **Now** the 75% of cash flow deals with one's discretionary Living Planning, and the winner here will have the professional edge.
- Here is where one must start off being conservative, and not speculative in nature. Then understand their individual risk tolerance, and always perform proper Due Diligence upon any business venture or financial investment.
- Speculation should be the last thought upon one's mind until they have established a solid foundation that will provide a hedge against inflation. Plus have adequate protection against any possible debt and credit risk issues.

This 25/75 disciplined planning is referred to as "Financial Success by Design." This concept has tested out and proved to be totally successful over time. There have been many, many wise and self-disciplined souls who have followed the rule of 25/75 in their successful business and professional life.

Well now! That **plus one's** own Social Security issue was going to be mentioned in the Government and Politician section, but I realized this illustration of fact should be presented here at the end. The following hopefully will make one aware of the Oop's!! The misuse and abuse of trust by both Republican and Democratic members of Congress over the years.

A great positive social security program that was, and is self-funded and self-sustaining; plus over the years had regularly adjusted deposits and percentages to reflect time value of money needs and benefits. So the following numbers should make the point of this issue. Now let's see reality by just using a middle of the road $50,000.00 annual income. This income number could represent one individual's income, or the combined income of an average couple.

First one must realize that Social Security is one of the greatest 401K type pension plans around. So on this $50,000.00 dollars . . .

The *EMPLOYER* matches ->	7.65% =	$3,825.00
The *EMPLOYEE* contributes	*7.65%* =	$3,825.00
Total per year: ->		**$7,650.00**

NOW with this deposit invested at 5% earning per year for 30 years, the total saving accumulation would be $533,872.00; all quite nice!

Invest from age 25 to age 65 would = **$805,854.00; all net/net!**

Then, if one invests this last number at 5% once one retires at age 65, this would yield annual income of $40,292.00 without ever touching the principal. **So Oop's!! - Where did all this money go?** *Particularly with the so-called unused mortality reserve accumulations all unspent when retirees died early at ages 63, 67, 69, or 73!?!?* Also, the widows benefit of $54,000.00 at age sixty, the average maximum potential orphan child benefits to age 16 of $268,000.00, the average spouse with children benefit of $384,000.00, and the average total Social Security Disability benefit for a person disabled over six months and longer of $462,000.00; still has a very little negative affect upon the Social Security's accumulation values.

Yes!! - Now there's this great political deception, con-job, and constructive fraud committed upon the American citizens by the majority membership of Congress; both Republican and Democrat. This deceptive Congress with ignorance turned a positive into a negative, and they now call Social Security a deficit liability. This now makes us creditors, and not investors. One hopefully sees now Mister and Misses blind public, that your $'s are not invested, but only borrowed by Congress and used irresponsibly by the general fund. Then they bless us all with only a callable note obligation with low value and returns to one's retirement, disability, and the widow's and children's benefit accounts.

Wow!! What a great benefit program that has been raped, pillaged and plundered by our representatives in Congress and their public employees, who do nothing but lie out of ignorance, and work to screw everyone born after 1960. Think it out, and please do your own math.

These political Social Security time bomb issues are <u>only</u> <u>*to*</u> ***create fog***, and have persons with no deep thinking or thought accepting an alternate reality of factitious non-factual distorted information. Fact is, our politicians are manipulating mathematics and law for their own self-serving benefits, but not to <u>*the your benefit*</u>.

#

EPILOGUE:

The effort was to show the road to get there, and the detours not to take.

The thought should be; "Be careful how you live, for you may be the only book some people ever read. 'Then be careful how you teach, for you may be the only lesson some pupils ever learn.' Therefore, what good is genius, - if it is not teachable or transferable?" This point is relevant because "we know not what the future holds, but we do know who holds the future. For ideals and principles continue from generation to generation. Not because they are right, but only when they are built into the hearts of the youth as they grow up."

The words of a song may say it best; "He was once a beautiful child of clay, who's to blame for what he is molded into today." So as a former Columbus, Ohio Mayor Sensenbrenner always used to say; "All the flowers of tomorrow are in the seeds of today, and we had better start fertilizing and cultivating today. For only the seedling youth become tomorrow's adult men and women who will lead us."

There was this nice picture page from Life Magazine that was all torn up into small pieces. There was a picture of the world on one side, and the face of a man on the other side. This little kid had quickly put the torn pieces back together again, with all the world pieces placed in the right order. The kid's father asked; "How did you do it so fast?" The kid responded; "When the face of the man was in place, the world was all right."

That is why the words of Louis Seltzer make sense; "I live for tomorrow, and I can scarcely wait until it comes. To be sure, yesterday was interesting. Of course, today is the immediate challenge. But tomorrow is for the plans, for the dreams, and for the reaching up." That is why there should be no sympathy for those who say: "I keep, I keep, I keep. I want, I want, I want. I need, I need, I need, but I do not want to pay; or to pay the price."

Reminds one of a retiring employee, who put in a memorable thirty years with his company. Actually only twenty-two years if you subtract coffee breaks.

There are two short poems that tend to remind one of losers, tag-a-long's, and not-my-problem sluffers. One is "Meddlesome Matty" written by Ann Taylor: "Besides, what can there be amiss; in opening such a box as this?" Then "Mr. Nobody" written by A. Anonymous: "He does his mis-chief,... though no one ever sees his face,... he tears the books,... leaves the door ajar,... puts damp wood upon the fire." This describes those people always envious of, and trying to interfere with one's success.

With friends like these who needs enemies? So in the world of finance and business, and in particularly with community charities; name these types of individuals the Chairman of the Board _Emeritus_. "E"- stands for you're out! & ***"meritus"*** means you deserved it. So while on the charity issue, the subject is often dealing with volunteers. Volunteers are mostly nice people, but not all of them. Be careful, for as a general rule, the people who want the job are too often the wrong people. For leadership, look for the person who is too busy, does not seem to have enough time, and is not seeking the job. This person quite often will be the best candidate with efficient time management, and quality effective leadership. Just because one volunteers does not mean they have adequate people skills or leadership capabilities, but they will make wonderful followers.

There is a wonderful spin advertizing method used in the circus to cover-up and white-wash an incident where there are the big spectacular three ring circus performances with trapeze acts, jugglers and high wire performers; as soon as an accident occurs, they blind side the audience and dazzle them by bring in the clowns. This calms the audience, some are deceived into thinking it was part of the act, and many times the accident is hardly ever noticed.

Bringing in the clowns is a nice business concept used many times by major business entities having market image difficulties. It is called advertizing to create a better market image, and to cover up their current or pending bad press. That is fine for big business, but for that person... _YOU_, the one sole individual that has an accident; who distracts and covers up for your misstep?

There are no clowns to cover-up your unfortunate incident should you appear as an "emperor with no clothes." This then is when one must really learn on cue to tap dance stage left, or tap dance stage right. This author can definitely prove out this point, and the point clearly debunks other's weak excuse for not preserving and progressing with personal success.

There are four (4) things in this life that you hopefully never want to encounter, or become familiar with. They are first spending thirty plus days strapped down on a striker bed, and being totally helpless and dependant upon others for all one's bodily needs. *Second*, having hartong prongs screwed into the side of the head, and dangling weights there from. *Third*, the surgery where they take bone off the hip to fix C5,6,7 in the neck. *Forth*, being fitted with a steel Halo head frame, screwed on and into the skull while fitted with a body cast. *Then* every thirty days having the doctor retighten the squeaky head screws of the halo deeper into the skull.

One would think that while having a well established and successful business operation that things could not get worst. Well think again! The word leaked out that this person was disabled, paraplegic, and would not ever be effective again as a Business, Estate and Economic Advisor (C.E.B.A.). Then two major financial corporations gave this thought-to-be disabled person, notice that all prior agreements were cancelled. Then one even with in-house assignment papers transferred over all clients immediately to their own captive employee representatives. The company immediately sent out their people to have all clients sign transfer papers stating that they were now the direct clients of the big corporation. Thankfully, only one client was lost due to the big corporation's unethical gamesmanship that backfired.

Worse yet, a trusted business lawyer, accountant, and business associate came to the bedside of this so-thought-to-be disabled person with a buyout agreement. The agreement stated that for a peanut/paltry sum of money, they would now be taking over all his clients and business operations. Nice try by one's so-called friends and phony appreciators, who reminded this person that you're only as good as your last sale. But this all turned out to be their wrong moves, particularly by the two big corporations. They all made one big glaring mistake; - this person recovered. He was upset yes, yet did not really get mad, but did get personal satisfaction, even though this author had to patiently wait twelve years before setting and springing the trap on one guilty party. They had a short memory, and this author had a long dormant memory, but was not losing any sleep at night.

So why did this author prevail? It was all based upon past consistent learning and yearning for knowledge, and observing and learning from everyone else's brilliant ideas. Along with learning one's key lessons well from life's experience, that were both good and bad; mostly from the memorable bad experiences. Then never forget one fact; the only winner will always be the one who comes out of the bear cave alive.

So let's appreciate some Shakespeare thoughts; . . .

> "One sin I know, another doth provoke;
> 'greed' as near to lust, as flame to smoke."
>
> "There are more things in heaven and earth,
> than are dreamt of in your philosophy."
>
> "Out, out, brief candle; - Life is but a
> walking shadow, a poor player, that
> struts and frets his hour upon the stage,
> and then is heard no more."

So let us remember Ralph Waldo Emerson again; "Fear not evil that has not yet arrived." And with Gustave Flauber; "Talent is a long patience." **Now** let's reconsider the conglomerate of thought with Harvey's Elwood P. Dowl; "You can be O'so cleaver, or O'so smart, - I recommend pleasant." **Then;** "I wrestled with reality for years; happily I finally won out over it."

Interesting! The word wrestle brings back to mind one of the more interestingly successful, talented, and sincere men of integrity that I've had the pleasure to know in this life. Well, to first know this person; one had to be a wrestler. Then one had to be wrestling in the final college conference match for the championship in the weight class. Well, stepping out onto the mat to face a blind wrestler was indeed interesting, for one had to keep making a noise so the blind wrestler knew where his opponent was located. At least there was no pin, and the blind wrestler won on points to be the champion in the weight class. But second place did not get this top opponent, who had already pinned three opponents in order to get to this final match, upon the recognition platform. This talented blind wrestler was the highlight of the total competition, and at the award ceremonies that evening in the university arena.

Then after college, the blind guy along with his blind wife opened up a small convenience store along with their two assistant employees 'Seeing Eye' dogs. They successfully operated this store in the community for years. They also devoted much of their free time tutoring children at the local blind school, and worked actively with the local blind Boy Scout and Girl Scout troops. I do not think anything else has to be said about these successful people, for their richness and wealth had nothing to do with money or property.

B11030
<u>donald jay denton</u>

"In my own little corner, in my own little chair, I can be whatever I want to be now." So let us now not forget, "Scaramouche."

*** * * Now a closing '<u>P.S'.</u> commentary for those <u>individualist</u> striving for success:**

Ah yes!! - Team work, team player, that's what is needed for achieving success; - <u>*Don't think so!*</u> This is group think, or committee rule.

Do not allow yourself to feel depressed, rejected or intimidated should someone tell you that you are not a team player. This may well be a subtle unrealized compliment, and a positive indication for your future potential success. Then of course, what type of team might they be talking about?

- A swim team is not similar to a basketball team
- A wrestling team is not similar to a football team.
- A track team is not similar to a baseball team.
- A bowling team is not similar to a hockey team.
- A <u>golf team</u> is not similar to a <u>soccer team</u>.

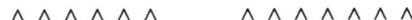

* Success based upon one's individual performance. The team lost, but one person got two first place awards.	* Other's mistakes can have one lose, for only the whole group wins or loses. No individual metals for one's good performance when the team loses.
Team 7 & 11	**Team 2 & 12**

Both teams had selected outstanding performers while obtaining great college scholarships. Some even advanced on into the Pro's. But in reality it has been noticed that more of the individualist winners on team 7 & 11 became successful business owners and professionals; even if a few came across as nerds with great individual talents. Known fact is that quite a few of these individualists successfully attended one of the top military academies. Also many of the others after college became very successful in life by the time they were in their forties.

Some very noticeable facts that the public very seldom noticed with members of *teams 7 & 11* are the shocking issues that seemingly continued to surround members of *teams 2 & 12*. Like low college graduation rates since many were academic risk and challenged, plus alcoholism, drug addiction, gambling addictions, robbery and assault convictions, business failures and personal bankruptcies. It has also been amazing how many have been ripped off by their business agents and financial advisors. Then by age fifty-five many seem to be burdened with mental or physical sports disabilities. Oop's!! Almost forgot murder, rape, group mayhem, animal cruelty, and spousal abuse. WOW! A real nice bunch of group think, low I.Q team players; where many played out their glorious college years while unable to read or write at a third grade level, or at all. A fact!

Now another large group of 2 & 12 sports hero's may have survived all these previous negatives, but ended up being errand boy front men for Investment firms, Real Estate firms, Energy firms, or Insurance companies. You could always spot them at business conferences or association conventions shaking hands and signing autographs, just to attract people to an exhibitor's booth. Their job was much like the organ grinder with a trained monkey on the end of their chain, just to solicit coin. Really quite sad for the *once famous, has been, hustling names of fame.*

The moral of this story might be for one to be very careful what type of a team they associate themselves with early on in this life. For persons when they are young (especially if a nerd, and not a jock) may not date the best looking person in high school or college. But quite often they will have the best looking chicks, cars, and homes at around age forty-five and beyond; plus a solid retirement with good financial security for life. The before mentioned comments are not meant to be a humorous joke, but a serious fact of reality that one had best take notice of early on in one's life.

So remember that paying the dues and the necessary price is just part of life's interesting game. ***Therefore, it is only as you wish it.*** So is it not strange that princes and kings, and clowns that caper in saw dust rings, and common folks like you . . . ?!?! Hope you know, and remember the rest.

So be diligent and wise to recognize that fame in any form does not equate into, or mean success. Particularly, should one surrender their integrity, their ethics, and their moral standards to infidelity, self-centered greed, and unethical social and business deceptions? Fact is, there is nothing more important for one's self recognition and peace of mind for true success in this life than fidelity, loyalty, honor, duty, to whatever true God, and Country.

"*Rosebud*"
 # - d.j.d.

#

www.ingramcontent.com/pod-product-compliance
Lightning Source LLC
Chambersburg PA
CBHW051536170526
45165CB00002B/759

* 9 7 8 1 4 6 3 5 2 1 1 2 7 *